on
Proust

Jean-François Revel

on Proust

Translated by
MARTIN TURNELL

THE LIBRARY PRESS
New York
1972

INTERNATIONAL STANDARD BOOK NUMBER
0-912050-10-1

LIBRARY OF CONGRESS CATALOG CARD NUMBER
70-161409

PRINTED IN THE UNITED STATES OF AMERICA

ACKNOWLEDGMENT

The publishers are grateful to Random House Inc. for permission to quote from the Scott Moncrieff translation of *Swann's Way*, *Within a Budding Grove*, *The Guermantes Way*, *Cities of the Plain*, *The Captive* and *The Sweet Cheat Gone*; and from the translation by Andreas Mayor of *The Past Recaptured* (entitled in England *Time Regained*).

Title, volume and page references are given for both the New York edition published by Random House and the London edition published by Chatto and Windus. The French edition of *A la Recherche du Temps Perdu* used here is the Pléiade edition.

Quotations from Montaigne are from Florio's translation.

102, 206

TABLE OF CONTENTS

FOREWORD

AT THE TIME I was writing this book I did not have the slightest intention of being drawn into the French controversies, which were just starting, about what became known as the "new criticism." The few and decidedly cursory references that I make in the last chapter to the different possible conceptions of literary criticism have no pretensions to be even an outline of the theoretical implications involved.

On the contrary, it was rather my intention to write the book in order to give myself a rest from theorising. Bergsonian, Marxist, existentialist and sociological criticism mixed up with, or at any rate containing, a certain dose of psychoanalysis coming from the schools of criticism of the 1950s, whose triumph had just about reached its peak or who were gasping for breath, was enough to fill a reader with a frantic desire to place the greatest possible distance between himself and their oppressive dogmatism and to seek refuge by concentrating on the text of original works. On the other hand, this statement does not in any way imply a proclamation in favor of the so-called "impressionist" criticism. I am of course sufficiently at home in the philosophical field to realise that it is impossible to escape completely from current ideologies. All I can say is that having re-read Proust's novel in its entirety after a first reading some fifteen years earlier, I was induced to comment in the most direct and straightforward manner possible on the observations which emerged from the re-reading.

There were occasions when my book was attacked in France on the ground that I apparently wanted to turn Proust into a "realist" or even a "naturalist," which would have meant moving in the opposite direction to the traditional metaphysic of Proust's French critics. It is a perfect example of the sort of incomprehension we find when a too academic brand of criticism is applied to texts in the fossilized categories. The misunderstanding is due to the fact that this kind of classification opposes in a summary fashion "realism" and "imaginative literature." Now it is sufficient to quote the example of Saint-Simon, who is both the greatest realist and at the same time one of the greatest visionaries in French literature, in order to see that this kind of opposition shows a complete failure to appreciate the infinite variety of literary creation and its method. It is tantamount to saying that Montaigne lacks inventiveness owing to the simple fact that it is his intention to confine himself to talking about what he believes to be true. One of the views that I have expressed in the book is that Proust invariably takes as his starting point something that he has seen and experienced at first hand and that he does not indulge in fancy.

THIS INTUITIVE SENSE that I have always had with literature was confirmed after the publication of my own study by George D. Painter's important biographical work. In this connection I venture to quote some passages from the review of the book that I wrote for *L'Express* when the French translation of the first volume was published.

"The great Proustian biography has appeared at last. The only previous and complete work on the subject, known as *Remembrance of Things Past*, appeared forty years earlier. The interest of this second biography lies in the fact that it confirms the autobiography of Marcel Proust or, if one prefers, is a confirmation that *Remembrance of Things Past* is truly an autobiography. Proust's art is to be found elsewhere than in the invention of events, characters, stories, feelings, dialogues, landscapes. It has now been proved by a day to day account of his life that he did not invent any of these things and that, as he himself has said, even when he amalgamates characters, places or situations, as he very often does, the elements of their amalgamation are real. The only story that Proust ever invented is that his book is a novel.

"But it needed a work as detailed as that of George D. Painter not simply to suggest, but to demonstrate the superimposition, which is so literal, so surprising, of actual experience and the story. It is a fact that Laure Hayman lived in the rue La Pérouse and that like Odette's her house had a door opening on to the rue Dumont-d'Urville; that Mme Straus when leaving home one evening to go to a fancy dress ball had in fact mistakenly put on black instead of red shoes, and the remark by the stupid lady-in-waiting, 'It can't snow any more; they've put down salt,' was really uttered by Princesse Mathilde's lady-in-waiting. *'Taquin le superbe'* (Taquin the proud) is a joke of Arthur Baignères'. The episode of Saint-Loup in his greatcoat took place at Weber's, and the Prince de Guermantes' obsession with the etiquette of the nobility comes from Aimery de La Rochefoucauld who explained his refusal to invite the Luynes by saying: 'They had no position in the year 1000.'

"It is true that the more important the characters are in *Remembrance of Things Past*, the more diverse are the sources from which they are derived. Charlus is at the same time, or rather successively, Montesquiou and Baron Doasan; Rachel is at the same time Mlle de Marsy and Louisa de Mornand; the Duchesse de Guermantes is in turn Mme de Chevigné, Mme Greffulhe and Mme Straus; Proust's grandmother used to read and quote Mme de Sévigné a good deal, but the story of her death in the novel was in reality that of his mother with a real Dr. du Boulbon.

"The core of the creation is never vague. The basis is always a given fact, too definite, too individualised, too unpredictable to be a complete invention.

"In the same way, already, in the pre-historic attempt at the biography of the young Proust by the young Proust, written before 1900, *Jean Santeuil*, 'all but three chapters of Part VI [as Painter says] are based with little alteration on Proust's holiday at Beg-Meil with Hahn in September–October 1895. But the telephone conversation with his mother in Chapter II is imported from the week with Lucien Daudet at Fontainebleau in October 1896,' etc. In *Remembrance of Things Past*, too, this event will frequently be contemporary with its literary expression and will all be relived by means of 'involuntary memory.'

"George Painter even goes so far as to attack one of the most venerated dogmas of literary history. According to him, Proust's homosexuality was not exclusive. The truth is that it is Proust himself who is the source of the dogma. We know from a famous passage in André Gide's *Journal* that he maintained 'that he had never loved women except spiritually and had never known love except with men.'

"Painter claims to have acquired some further information on the point, which interests him, through going back to sources which would demonstrate sexual relations with women. Proust, he says, did not invariably use men as his models for the *'jeunes filles en fleurs'* (young girls in bloom), Gilberte and Albertine; quite the contrary. Painter seems to us to be both right and wrong. He is right when he says that in *Remembrance of Things Past* there is an intuitiveness and a love of femininity which rules out the view that all the young girls and all the young women whom the narrator loves are boys in disguise. He is also right when he demolishes the procedure of the metaphysical critics who, while rejecting the whole of the realistic content of the novel and proclaiming that it is autonomous, make use of biographical elements which are unconvincing in order to argue that in the case of the narrator as such homosexuality is there in principle though he never attributes it to himself. But Painter seems to us to be wrong when he treats some very minor incidents, which he mentions in this context, as decisive proof of sexual love with women.

"The incidents are proof of nothing more than the spiritual loves that Proust spoke about to Gide or the *amitié amoureuse* (romantic friendship) that, as she herself said, Louisa de Morn- and felt for Proust. Now in the second volume of his biography Mr. Painter seems to take for granted a liaison with Louisa de Mornand because the actress visited Proust's home several times and because he sent her a little poem.

"But he does not mention Reynaldo Hahn as a possible and partial model for both Odette and Albertine—something which from the *Correspondence* appears obvious. In other words, for Mr.

Painter the fact that Proust had meetings with young women always seems proof that he went to bed with them while the fact that he went to bed with men hardly seems proof that he had meetings with them.

"According to Mr. Painter's perfect formula, *Remembrance of Things Past* is in every way a 'creative autobiography.' And the demonstration he gives is an excellent opportunity for ridding ourselves of the academic conception of imagination which is a hindrance to present day literary criticism because it is based on the assumption that imagination would always be the negation of something actually seen.

"The Proustian imagination is not a faculty that carries us away from reality: it helps us to see it. In the case of Proust there is no antinomy between 'biographical criticism' and interpretation by means of the artist's 'interior world.' For this interior world is no more than a roundabout way of achieving a better view of a truth which is inseparable from beauty. It was through Ruskin that Proust took cognizance of this function of imagination. 'The poet,' said Ruskin, 'is a sort of scribe writing at the dictation of nature; the writer's duty is not to imagine [in the sense of "complete invention"], but to perceive reality.' 'And since duty is infinitely more important than life,' Proust goes on, 'its accomplishment will bring salvation.'

"All the same, I cannot agree with Mr. Painter when, understandably irritated by the conventional explanations of Proust's work, he writes: 'What do they know of *A la Recherche* who only *A la Recherche* know?' To subscribe to this view would amount to a declaration that Proust failed as a writer. If it is true that the literary historian cannot hope to understand the genesis of *Remembrance of Things Past* without knowing about the life of the man who wrote it, it would be a contradiction to assert, unless we are to decree Proust's artistic failure, that the simple reader cannot understand by merely reading the novel what the narrator wanted to say to him."

Painter's work has been somewhat coolly received by Proustologues for reasons which have rather more to do with a facile conformism than a concern for historical truth or a proper understanding of literature. As for myself, my own ambition, which was rather more modest, was to liberate the reader, and for very good reasons to begin by liberating myself, from that asphyxiating climate which helps to create the atmosphere of the confessional and to diffuse an odor of the sacristy round one of the most open and most vital works of the twentieth century.

*   *   *

I HAD ALWAYS INTENDED to take advantage of a new edition of this book by adding a chapter which would give consideration to critical theories which have been put forward since it was first published in 1960. When the time came, however, I realised that it would mean writing another book and that simply to graft a chapter on to the present work would be a mistake. What I have tried to do, as I have suggested, is to make some observations in the margin of a reading of *Remembrance of Things Past* without anything more, and not to make pronouncements of my own on the nature of criticism.

The last chapter in particular, like the others, is about Proust. It assembles a number of comments on the conception of the work of art that we find *in Proust* and not on "the essence" of the work of art considered in itself.

In the same way, I have not tried to use Proust in order to illustrate this or that ephemeral theory of literature. I have been criticized, for example, for making him far too much of a sociologist. If I had written in the first post-war decade, I should have been criticized for not making him enough of a sociologist. What is more, at a time when exaggerated attention is being paid to structural problems in literature, there were hostile reactions to the view that *Remembrance of Things Past* was not "composed"— as *Ulysses* was—in accordance with some formal, rigid and, so to speak, plastic model, but was fashioned by a series of creative additions—a fact which has since been confirmed by the work done on the manuscripts.

In both cases the reactions were governed by "models" of what might be described as social material or formal imagination in literature. We cannot, as I have said, deny the sociological slant of Saint-Simon's *Memoirs*, which does not mean that anyone is contesting the fact that they are a literary phenomenon. Nor can we deny their "form," but this does not mean that literary form is always based on some sort of spatial scheme and can always be fitted into a synoptic table. That is the most simplified form in existence. Fortunately, there are others. The truth is that we must be on our guard not so much against the method of explanation as its claim to dominate and above all its style: an academic sociological explanation fills me with the same horror as an academic structuralist explanation of Saint-Simon or Proust.

No system of literary criticism has ever been retained by posterity. We might go further and say that every system of literary criticism necessarily looks like the obligatory butt of the generation which follows and is without any hope of being given another chance. The Faguets of today make fun of the Faguets of yesterday, comfortably installed in the very vehicle which is in the process of carrying them like their predecessors to the guillotine. Great works, like those queens who regularly had last night's lover executed at daybreak, are punctual in laying out their periodical ration of stone cold critical corpses.

The sight of earlier critical systems going down the drain does not worry the creators of later systems any more than the disappearance of a political régime worries the instigator of the *coup d'état* which founds the new régime. In politics, it is never a matter of knowing if the changes in the price of gold were better or less well explained under the previous régime, but simply of being the person whose job it is at present to provide explanations.

It is probable that a system of literary criticism is much more a protective than a penetrative system. Once the system has done its job for a couple of generations, the machine comes to a halt. It is characteristic of any system of literary criticism that it makes all the works to which it is applied resemble one another. Since art is the reign of difference, it is a matter of smoothing out disturbing differences in which not a single fragment is or should be dependent on the same language.

That is why people are perpetually demanding with untiring naïveté the creation of a critical language. "What we lack," the critics write, "is a language." Not at all! It is precisely the one thing that they do not lack.

A system of literary criticism which makes all works resemble one another is therefore an expression of the narcissism of the person who writes and he appeals to the narcissism of his followers. Literary need is not very widespread; the need to experience literary need, on the other hand, is very widespread. It is necessary therefore to provide those who do not feel it with a substitute for literary need.

Literature, which is created by and for people who are ill-adapted (to themselves, to others, and to the community), is eventually salvaged as an instrument of adaptation.

A man who adapts himself to literature does not need literature. On the contrary, he needs criticism. If to free oneself from literature—that malady of language—consists in linking one literary work to another, that is the critic's mission. The less fond one is of it, the more militant one's behavior. Criticism, which is the work of tireless go-betweens (but what turncoat ever tires?) and good little soldiers who are immediately mown down by machine-gun fire (but a night out in Paris will put all that right), sets out to maintain a "literary" surface agitation and to translate into the terms of this surface agitation the works of the past promoted to the honor of providing sauce for the specialists of the day.

Critical systems are constructed in order to satisfy the excruciating absence of curiosity about literary works which is known as the thirst for culture.

Naïve people always imagine that one has at last found the right way of never missing a literary work of value.

Antisthenes advised his disciples against learning to read. He was right. Reading can never be taught.

I

French literature is indebted to the visits that Marcel Proust made here for *Within a Budding Grove* which is a veritable synthesis of beach life at the beginning of the century. Albertine played at diabolo on the jetty; her granddaughters go in for jokari. Christian names, games and fashions change, but the Norman beaches will always spell happiness for youth.

> (*Les* Guides Michelin Régionaux,
> *Fascicule* Normandie, *Article* Cabourg)

La verité et la vie sont bien ardues, et il me restait d'elles, sans qu'en somme je les connusse, une impression où la tristesse était peut-être encore dominée par la fatigue.

Truth and life are very arduous, and I retained without really knowing them, an impression where sadness was perhaps still dominated by fatigue.

> PROUST, *La Fugitive* (*The Sweet Cheat Gone*)

Chapter I

PROUST AND LIFE

REMEMBRANCE OF THINGS PAST is one of the most homogeneous books in existence. It is the work of a writer whose maturity completely dominates what he says; who could say a great deal more, or say it differently; who does not "boast," but to whom everything that he relates—or the equivalent—has actually happened; and lastly, who explains a thing not because of a taste for theory, but because he honestly believes that he understood it in that way and does not imagine that there is much chance of putting it better later on. A homogeneous book, indeed, but at the same time only up to a certain point because we sometimes have the impression that Proust incorporates into his present thought, translated into the terms of the mature man—conferring on them in this way an authority and a weight that they did not perhaps possess originally—ideas conceived, developed and recited in the depths of his being at every period of his life. The adult work seems to be the ultimate findings of a long meditation of a more or less voluntary nature, often interrupted, completely subjected to the moods of a man capable of insisting for hours on end on the same point, the same circumstance, the same portrait; saying them over to himself, composing them for himself, writing them in his head, without having to make any effort to concentrate on his subject, but on the contrary being hooked by reality.

This particular facility does not make the difficulty that Proust experienced in settling down to write inexplicable: a difficulty which was not of course the result of lack of material, but was caused by the failure to find easily a common rhythm which fitted the flow of his thought and the organisation of daily life. His problem was the problem of making a start: not the start of each page, but of the book as a whole. Once the work has begun, he swings backwards and forwards in it; sentences write themselves, overflowing on all sides, emerging from one another, and the difficulty becomes much more a matter of interrupting himself, breaking off. The development swarms with new scenes, features, sorties, maxims, general conclusions which in fact conclude nothing, but lead to fresh developments. Like Montaigne, Proust only thinks when he is able to think without making an effort, think to satiety, and he becomes in spite of himself obsessed with his own ideas.

He must always have thought in this way, at length and often, which explains the prodigious interest he manages to take in boring parties. For it is not the boredom of these parties that he observes; it is himself, staggered to find, when he reads the pastiche of the Verdurins' salon in the Goncourt manner in *The Past Recaptured*, that he has seen none of the things he was supposed to see, that everything that strikes other people has escaped him.

What is the reason? Goncourt is taken up with the opinions and theories of Mme Verdurin; Proust with her manner of laughing. Goncourt admires the Verdurins' china; Proust the way in which the Verdurins talk about their admirable china. In this way he places himself on the level where what might be called the nervous system behind events makes it appear as though he is looking closely at a picture in a strong light. The eye fixes on the over-elaborate treatment, the brush marks, the repainting, whereas when he takes an ordinary straight look at it he only sees what is the first coat of an illusion to which art criticism will add a second. It follows that Proust views things simultaneously under two different aspects: men's behavior and the explanations they give of it; their conscious but un-acknowledged intentions; the motives and impulses which, un-known to themselves, are at the root of their actions. Finally (it is perhaps the most important point of all), there are the mo-ments when their actions begin to live, so to speak, on their own account, becoming independent of men and detaching themselves from them in order to perform a ballet consisting of gesture and intonation which creates the impression that, without knowing it, every man gives of himself. There is Legrandin who, as a result of frequenting places of ill-fame and his fear of being seen entering or leaving them, has contracted the habit of no longer crossing a threshhold, even to enter a salon, except like a gust of wind and by a sort of bound designed to blot out or hide himself; the Duc de Guermantes clinging obstinately to the hand of the narrator's father *"pour bien lui prouver qu'il ne lui marchandait pas le contact de sa chair précieuse* (in order to prove . . . that he made no bargain about my father's right to the privilege of contact with the ducal flesh),"[1] a gesture into which he thought he was putting a whole world of greatness of soul and which obviously inconveniences the beneficiary; Proust himself who, even before reflecting on it, acquiesces mechanically when M. de Charlus reproaches him with "dilettantism." Dilettantism is the error which the baron regards as the main cause of the 1914 war.

> *Par surprise du reproche, manque d'esprit de repartie, déférence envers mon interlocuteur, attendrissement pour son amicale bonté, je répondis comme si, ainsi qu'il m'y invitait, j'avais aussi à me frapper la poitrine, ce qui était parfaitement stupide, car je n'avais pas l'ombre du dilettantisme à me reprocher.*
>
> From astonishment at the reproach, from lack of readiness in repartee, from deference towards my interlocutor, and also because I was touched by his friendly kindness, I replied as though I too, as he suggested, had cause to beat my breast—an idiotic reaction, for I had not the shadow of dilettantism to reproach myself with.[2]

When we look straight through the celluloid at the film of *Remembrance of Things Past* without projecting it, or when we pass it slowly through the excellent movieola, which is the index of the Pléiade edition, we are struck by the number of short sequences, complete in themselves, out of which it is constructed. Sometimes they are visual: *"Bloch était entré en sautant comme une hyène* (Bloch had come bounding into the room like a hyena)."[3]

[1] II, p. 33; *The Guermantes Way*: I, pp. 366–7 (RH); V, p. 35 (C&W).
[2] III, p. 808; *The Past Recaptured*: p. 86 (RH); pp. 146–7 (C&W).
[3] III, p. 966; *The Past Recaptured*: p. 207 (RH); p. 360 (C&W).

Sometimes aural, imposing a certain intonation on the reader's ear: "*On disait: 'Mais, vous oubliez, un tel est mort,' comme on eût dit 'Il est décoré,' 'il est de l'Académie'* (I heard people say, 'But you forget that so-and-so is dead,' exactly as they might have said 'he has a decoration' or 'he has been elected to the Academy')."[1] Whether audiovisual or purely visual, the snapshot acquires from the start the vivacity of an epitome, the narrative potential encased in the kind of immobility of the image that we find in an engraving by Goya, Daumier or simply Gavarni, or, more agreeably, Constantin Guys, whether it is a scene of sadistic love at Montjouvain between Mlle Vinteuil and her girl friend—a scene viewed in its entirety in the luminous framework of a lighted window at night time—or whether it is the features, at once comic and hideous, of M. de Norpois, the arrival of M. de Charlus at Mme Verdurin's at La Raspelière, or again the majestic attitude of M. Bloch, the father:

> *N'allant pas jusqu'à avoir une voiture, M. Bloch louait à certains jours une victoria découverte a deux chevaux de la Compagnie, et traversait le bois de Boulogne, mollement étendu de travers, deux doigts sur la tempe, deux autres sous le menton, et si les gens qui ne le connaissaient pas le trouvaient à cause de cela "faiseur d'embarras," on était persuadé dans la famille que, pour le chic, l'oncle Salomon aurait pu en remontrer à Gramont–Caderousse.*

> Not going to the length of having a carriage of his own, M. Bloch used on special occasions to hire an open victoria with a pair of horses from the Company, and would drive through the Bois de Boulogne, his body sprawling limply from side to side, two fingers pressed to his brow, other two supporting his chin, and if people who did not know him concluded that he was "an old nuisance," they were all convinced in the family, that for smartness Uncle Solomon could have taught Gramont-Caderousse a thing or two.[2]

A pencil sketch for which the second part of the sentence serves as a caption. Or lastly, whether it is a matter, once again in the Bois de Boulogne, of the profile entirely in light colors of Mme Swann appearing in the Allée des Acacias.

---

[1] III, p. 977; *The Past Recaptured*: p. 216 (RH); p. 375 (C&W).
[2] I, p. 722; *Within a Budding Grove*: I, p. 583 (RH); IV, p. 97 (C&W).

PROUST WANTS TO SEE phenomena as they are in themselves; he is deeply convinced that they are in fact exactly as he sees them, we might almost say as he *receives* them. For the lack of interest he displays, during a dinner, in matters which to him are superficial, but which captivate Goncourt, is a sign that in his case receptivity is confined to things which in his eyes are important and the perception of which gives him the certainty of being in contact with reality as it is in itself. The certainty of reaching the heart of things by making himself adaptable, by turning his eyes in a manner which makes him accessible to the images conveyed to him by the inner substance of the real with its truth, its laws—this certainty emerges clearly from the following comparison between optical instruments:

> *Bientôt, je pus montrer quelques esquisses. Personne n'y comprit rien. Même ceux qui furent favorables à ma perception des vérités que je voulais graver dans le temple, me félicitèrent de les avoir découvertes "au microscope," quand je m'étais au contraire servi d'un télescope pour apercevoir des choses, très petites en effet, mais parce qu'elles étaient situées à une grande distance, et qui étaient chacune un monde. Là où je cherchais les grandes lois, on m'appelait fouilleur de détails.*

> Before very long I was able to show a few sketches. No one understood anything of them. Even those who commended my perception of the truths which I wanted eventually to engrave within the temple, congratulated me on having discovered them "with a microscope", when on the contrary it was a telescope that I had used to observe things which were indeed very small to the naked eye, but only because they were situated at a great distance, and which were each one of them in itself a world. Those passages in which I was trying to arrive at general laws were described as so much pedantic investigation of detail.[1]

The author of *Remembrance of Things Past* is not only invaded by the presence of things and scenes; we have the impression, as he himself says, that he has always felt that he cannot stop himself from describing them carefully in words. In fact, we frequently have the feeling in *Remembrance of Things Past* that we are faced with "set pieces" without my intending that there should be

[1] III, p. 1041; *The Past Recaptured*: p. 266 (RH); p. 463 (C&W).

anything pejorative about the expression because it is obviously
a preparation in depth. Proust is capable of taking up the same
story again in a hundred different ways with the same verve and
conviction, and in fact he often does it. The intimate contact
with the thing to be said engenders the need and the talent for
describing it several times without repeating himself. Proust
has contemplated this reality for a long time; he has undoubtedly
thought hundreds of times about a conversation, an individual,
an episode, has impregnated them, in his head, with his words
and sentences, already *expressing* them, finding one, sometimes
a dozen, forms of expression; composing, ordering, classifying
his formulas, forgetting them, but not wishing to lose per-
manently the possibility of going back to their source. It may be
that it is here that we come across one of the reasons for his
remorse at not having written in the course of the long years of
idleness—a remorse which seems to have come from the simple
fear of dying without having *taken note*, at the very time when the
events which he is relating occurred; taken note, not of the
events themselves (he never fails to do that!) but of his own
words and also of the ideas and moral reflections that these
events suggested to him. Without this form of mental pre-
writing, we should not understand the nature of the photo-
graphy so marvelously to the point of certain Proustian passages:
the manner in which Charlus, without appearing to do so, be-
comes absorbed in the contemplation of Mme de Surgis-le-Duc's
two sons playing cards; or the way in which Swann, almost a
dying man, is overcome for the last time by desire as he bends
down over the corset of this same Mme de Surgis (and Proust
fastens on Swann's fleeting look in which the love of woman that
dominated his life comes into collision in his eyes with the idea
of imminent death); or again, the Molièresque portrait of Pro-
fessor Dieulafoy who specialises in confirming that the patient
is in his death agony or is dead. Proust must have thought often
of these mini-portraits and so many other archetypes before
writing them down, less in order to have them ready-made and
at hand than to have them ready for making—in order to feel,
when he thought about them and was making preliminary

sketches, that he *could* sit down at any moment he might choose and put them into writing.

This explains the dual character, the dual savor of his work, in which the fruits of a slow process of preparation end by ripening and which nevertheless possesses the ease and relaxation of complete spontaneity. Proust improvises his fancies: he is not exactly a reporter (we remember his contempt for "observation" which for him meant putting things short-sightedly under one's nose and making a "note" because one was incapable of seeing them) nor exactly a man of imagination because he is only interested in things which have really happened. The fact that, in comparison with the attention demanded by the present, for him memory is favorable to the intense vision and feeling of the event, does not mean that it is anything but the event itself, the event alone, lived through, which interests him. For Proust memory is never an illusion, the mystical embellishment and flight of romantics from ungrateful life. On the contrary, it is the present which is illusory and blurred for reasons that are entirely concrete: distractions, conversations, fatigue and, above all, complacency which owing to the need for the euphoria of the moment, makes us exaggerate the qualities of our interlocutors. It follows that the literary purification of the scene takes place in memory because in reality memory is the present, but is free from draughts, from the vanity of trying to dazzle and the anguish of love. A mist melts away; the object emerges; an image is formed; a scene takes shape or, more often, a conspectus of gestures and intonations which can eventually be ascribed to several different people and play the part of those little portable diptyches in early Flemish painting that travelers opened at each of their stopping places.

Pictures of this kind are continually turning up all through *Remembrance of Things Past*. Thus the passage describing the slimming down of the aging Legrandin contrasted with the fattening of Charlus—"the opposite effects of the same vice"—is applied word for word to Saint-Loup in the same way as the passage about people entering like a gust of wind owing to their

habit of crossing *ex abrupto* the threshhold of a shady hotel. The
fact that Proust did not have time to revise *The Past Recaptured*
and remove these repetitions enables us to show that these forms
of behavior and these profiles were already written down men-
tally and were used twice because the catch of the machine was,
so to speak, released twice by mistake. In the same way, the
description of Gilberte appearing at table, "painted up to the
eyes," the same evening that her husband comes to dinner in
order to try to re-seduce him is literally re-applied to the
Princesse de Guermantes, who wanted to seduce Charlus (!),
in the admirable unpublished section which fortunately has
been included at the end of Volume II of the Pléiade edition.[1]

Nothing is more effective in verifying the existence of these
starting points, these scenes which had become "classic" in
Proust's internal system of mimetics before he had even begun
to write them down; nothing is more revealing than the sub-
titles that he had used for the different parts of *Remembrance of
Things Past*. For example, at the beginning of the second part of
Guermantes Way we read: "My grandmother's illness—Bergotte's
illness—The Duke and the Doctor—Decline and death of my
grandmother." Now, if we compare the schema with its realiza-
tion, the original sketches do not breathe a word about passages
which in the final version will sometimes be the longest and
most important (so in the volume quoted, the evening at the
Opera, the stay at Doncières, the afternoon party at Mme de
Villeparisis's). Inversely, a number of scenes announced in
advance are not handled at all or scarcely handled, but will turn
up elsewhere ("Bergotte's illness"), or perhaps will become a
detail in a much longer episode ("The Duke and the Doctor"),
or they may be related in a different light ("The wit of the
Guermantes, as displayed before the Princesse de Parme" be-
comes in fact something like "I shed my illusions about the
Guermantes and judge the world"). Or, again, they appear in a
different order from the one announced. There is sometimes a
displacement of pictures previewed (and viewed) in relation to
developments and growths when the full story comes pouring

[1] III, p. 702 and II, p. 1185.

out. At other times, on the contrary, there is a precise incor-
poration of one of the pictures in the dimension already an-
nounced in the general unfolding of the story: "A strange visit
to M. de Charlus" points to the "number" already put together
long ago. Its brilliant success is visible in all its effects, in the way
it has dwelt on and repeated each of its discoveries—measured,
purified and fiddled with a crazy pleasure the droll progression
and the indescribable "star turns"—and how many times
Proust says: "at the moment when this was happening, I began
to think that, I started to reflect that," when he comes to the
irrevocable establishment or the obvious explanation of a
phenomenon which has always interested him. He tells us not
what the author is thinking now, at the moment of writing his
book, but what the narrator himself thought long ago and made
clear to himself. Even if his opinion has not changed, it is im-
portant that it should be expressed in the way in which it was
experienced at the time of the event. The reflections, however
generalised, form part of the narration, are linked to the situa-
tion as reported, to the man himself who was one of the actors
playing a part in the situation. It is this that is too often lost
sight of when we seek to isolate Proust the theorist. Proust's
ideas are inseparable from "things seen," from mobile tableaux,
which are the basic cells of *Remembrance of Things Past* and show
that the remembrance of things past began in the present.

It is easier to see that the order in which these mobile
tableaux will finally be shown is not itself essential, that strictly
speaking there is no such thing as a Proustian narrative thread,
by studying the announcement of the work "to appear in 1914,"
which was printed on the fly-leaf of the original edition, rather
than the final table of contents:

To appear in 1914:

Remembrance of Things Past

The Guermantes Way

At Mme Swann's—Country Names: country—First Sketches
of Baron Charlus and R. de Saint-Loup—Names of people: the
Duchesse de Guermantes—The Salon of Mme de Villeparisis.

Remembrance of Things Past

The Past Recaptured

In the Shadow of Young Girls in Bloom—The Princesse de
Guermantes—M. de Charlus and the Verdurins—The "Virtues
and Vices"—Marriage of R. de Saint-Loup—Perpetual Adoration.

THERE IS A PICTURE of Max Ernst's which when seen at a
distance looks like a map of Europe, but which as soon as it is
seen at close quarters shows that it is not composed of any form
really belonging to Europe and at the same time cannot be any-
thing except a map of Europe: it is *Europe after the Rain*; and as
often happens with Max Ernst, reading the title soothes the
malaise caused by the picture itself.

Does it not look as though we are concerned with something
like "Remembrance of Things Past after the Rain," although in
contrary fashion it is a sort of tertiary era in the Proustian
geology? In the same way, when we consider the state of our
continent in an ancient geological period, we see oceans in
places where today we find mountain ranges and inversely. So
we observe that of Proust's plans everything has survived in one
form or another, but not in the same place, not in the same
relationship with the rest, and not given the same relief. Some-
thing which ought to weigh a ton is eventually reduced to a few
ounces and replaced by elements not foreseen in the programme,
but destined to fill a large part of the horizon. *Within a Budding
Grove* placed after *The Guermantes Way* and turning into a simple
episode of *The Past Recaptured*; Mme de Cambremer placed on
the same level of importance as Charlus and Saint-Loup, the
"virtues and the vices" of Padua and Combray—meaning, I
suppose, the visit to the Arena and the confrontation with the
memory of the reproductions offered by Swann—which were
announced as a whole chapter and will only take up a few lines
in *The Sweet Cheat Gone*; finally, the complete absence of Alber-
tine—that configuration of *Things Past*, at this stage of its evolu-
tion, so different from the forms and proportions that will be
assumed by the adult organism, allows us to appreciate or to
suspect the respective roles played, in the case of Proust the

writer, by the improvisator who creates abundantly and by the obsessed person who reproduces a number of scenes which it is impossible to modify.

With Proust, writing is the result of the need to express certain definite things, to relate a particular story and no other. His talent is not an undifferentiated disposition which individualizes itself in a subject or category of subjects. He is driven on by his subjects; he does not choose them and resembles those travelers who in the past became writers simply because they were the only witnesses of extraordinary things in Oceania or the Antarctic. That is why in appearance Proust's writing is so careless, why he prefers to go on writing instead of making corrections, why he makes endless additions, rewrites without replanning, overcharges, forgets, repeats himself, upsets the form. It is not because he improvises, but on the contrary because he does not improvise and is carried away by his material. The writer who improvises effectively, that is to say, who comes across his ideas at the moment of writing them down, is far too frightened of losing the thread to allow himself such exterior disorder because when one invents on the spot one is not sure, as Proust is, of seeing the complete resurgence, in one place or another, of something which has not been noted, developed, put into its proper place. Proust is certainly afraid of not having the opportunity of putting himself to work, but once he has done so, once he has joined the n+1 of external conditions, psychological or physiological, without which he is unable to work, he knows that his themes cannot melt away, and that only illness or death could prevent him from finishing his work. Once his problem— not lack of ideas, but the difficulty of getting down to work in a material sense—is solved, he knows that whatever happens he must take account of such-and-such a fact, conception, metaphor. With him composition, as little separated as possible from the very substance of the facts related, is embedded in the fibre of the work and is inescapable.

There has been a lot of talk about the subtlety of Proust's composition. It has been compared at various times to serial music, to a generalised relativity, to undulatory mechanism and

to the quantum theory—the list of scientific equivalents being
necessarily limited by the cursory information provided by the
manuals of logic used in the philosophy class. It would therefore
give the impression of cultivating platitude and a paradox at the
same time if we observed the extent to which the composition of
Remembrance of Things Past is loose without much in the way of
calculation or rhythm. It is obvious that Proust does not com-
pose, does not "put together as a whole," in the architectural
sense of the term, elements defined in view of this very con-
struction. It is in any case something that only bad writers do.
Moreover, it seems clear, after a single reading of *Remembrance
of Things Past*, that as the book moves forward, the process is one
of decomposition rather than composition, that it is enriched by
swelling in size, by overflows and local hypertrophies like
Montaigne's *Essays*. The conjunction of ideas and pictures,
worked out in advance, is quickly swallowed up in an enormous
mass which in a way has grown up as a result of additions. The
manner in which the work is executed goes far beyond the
original conception, as we can see from Proust's own announce-
ment of what was to follow *Swann's Way*. On one side there
persists, though in a considerably attenuated form, the impro-
visation conceived by the author who wanted to put down on
paper some obsessive memories, but who being obscurely con-
scious that these memories would always re-emerge—as the
psychoanalyst knows that the theme of which his patient has
lost the thread will re-emerge—abandons at every turn the main
line, takes the liberty of plunging into the longest of digressions.
And it is the continual return, although more and more widely
spaced, that gives *Remembrance of Things Past* its melodies and its
counterpoints, which could prompt people to speak of "clever"
composition (as *Swann's Way* begins with some one going to bed
and ends with some one getting up). On the other hand, and
more and more generously as the book becomes what it is,
another form of improvisation is used in the service of the verifi-
cation of thought and written in the present tense: it is the impro-
visation of digressions which envelop and drown the basic images
and finishes by making both ourselves and the author lose sight

of them. As with Montaigne, the digression becomes the most voluminous, perhaps the most significant and, from the literary point of view, the best part of the book. Although Proust remains convinced that he is dealing with the essentials of his own personality in his ancient themes, there can be no doubt on the contrary that it is the digressions which saved him from his obsessions.

I HAVE NOT ATTEMPTED in the preceding pages to deal with the historical genesis of Proust's work. The feelings that I have expressed are based solely on Proust's text and, indeed, on a careful reading of the one and only *Remembrance of Things Past* since it remains true that, in spite of the interest of the unpublished writings which have appeared in recent years, "Proust is a one-book man," as Bernard de Fallois put it[1]—confirmation of the fact that Proust's genius is bound up with one form of material only, that it is not a question of manner.

I am not embarking on the question of the relation between Proust's book and his biography of which I only know the things that nobody can help knowing. The Proustologues must forgive me if I speak, without distinguishing between them, of "Proust" and "the narrator." Although according to Proust himself there is no complete and literal incorporation of any real person and any actual event in the book, it seems to me equally beyond discussion that nothing, absolutely nothing, in it is pure creation and that the author never speaks in it except about what he has experienced or seen. Whether it consists of imaginary memories or is a genuine work of fiction or the two together, the deepest concern in *Remembrance of Things Past* is for reality. By making fun of a down-to-earth aesthetic of mere "observation," of the laborious process of transposition, Proust naïvely imagined that he had brought to book realism or even reality. But whatever may have been the pulling to pieces, the arrangements, the dispersals, the plastic reconstructions that he inflicted on the basic elements of his story, we may wonder whether he invented a single one of these elements.

[1] Preface to *Contre Sainte-Beuve* (1954), p. 10. (This important preface was left out of the English version. *Tr.*)

16

ON PROUST

It is certainly not accurate to say that Proust "pours" his own "experience of life" into the novel because one does not notice one fine day that one has "experience." And besides, how can we place this day? Would it not be necessary to push it back indefinitely towards the time of one's birth? In reality, experience is not something that is acquired (how many people have returned from prison camps just as *petits-bourgeois* as they were before) or, at any rate, when it is acquired, it belongs to all time and one reflects on it for all time. Proust himself denounced the illusion that there exist in life "minutes of truth" which are provoked by exceptional "moments":

> *Car il est extraordinaire à quel point, chez les rescapés du feu que sont les permissionnaires, chez les vivants ou les morts qu'un médium hypnotise ou évoque, le seul effet du contact avec le mystère soit d'accroître, s'il est possible, l'insignifiance des propos.*
>
> For it is extraordinary how, in the survivors of battle, which is what soldiers on leave are, or in living men hypnotised or dead men summoned by a medium, the only effect of contact with mystery is to increase, if that be possible, the insignificance of the things people say.[1]

Thus the idea of becoming conscious of the meaning and the possibility of his work—when in *The Past Recaptured* Proust waits for the piece of music to finish before making his way into the salon of Mme Verdurin who is now the Princess de Guermantes —this sudden "revelation" has always seemed to me to be a somewhat deliberate version of the events. I will go so far as to say that it has always seemed to me to be a good example of what is known of "ideological superstructure." What is more, in the place where it appears, the revelation so often announced is not a novelty. *The Past Recaptured*, indeed, contains nothing but repetitions on this point. Proust has already explained a hundred times what he himself regarded a being the source of literary "creation," as he calls it. Yet people go on repeating confidently that *The Past Recaptured* is the key to the work. Now *The Past Recaptured* is a delightful collection of memories of Paris in time of war, a salutary satire on chauvinism, on nationalist

[1] III, p. 757; *The Past Recaptured*: p. 47 (RH); p. 79 (C&W).

salons, the patriotic Egerias, the press filled with the martial prose of the Norpois and the Brichots. A substantial part of the book is devoted to a chronicle, in the form of an hors-d'oeuvre of the homosexual evolution of Saint-Loup and the drama behind the Gilberte-Saint-Loup marriage. We find at the end what is known, in the language of the Sorbonne, as some extremely "precious" data about the conditions in which Proust went to work, battling simultaneously against illness and his habits; about his indifference to the judgement of other people on the value of his work, or at any rate their immediate judgement. In it we read once again the account of his last visit to the outside world, that afternoon party at which everybody gave the impression of "looking glum" as a result of growing old. Finally and above all, we are aware not so much of Charlus's masochistic Grand Guignol séance during the night in the shady hotel—a restful but slightly conventional entertainment—as of the admirable meeting between Proust and Charlus on the boulevard. What a sublime monologue the baron's is on the war, the Germans, history, the mistakes of French in Norpois's articles, the period, the dilettantism and the sad impossibility, owing to the position in which events have placed him, of sending his usual annual greetings to his cousin, Francis-Joseph etc.[1] As for the revelation of the nature and meaning of the work, which had already been superabundantly explained in *Swann's Way* and which the author receives here from the resurgence in his memory of the sense of the unequalness of the level of the flagstones of St. Mark's in Venice, it is perhaps the least inspired passage in *The Past Recaptured* and the least unexpected.[2] Moreover, the nature of the lightning illumination bringing the work to the world would be comprehensible if it were a mystical poem or a metaphysical ecstasy coming at every turn in the course of everyday life. But this revelation is more surprising in its prophetic incandescence when we see later that what it really amounts to is a minute description of the head waiters at hotels

[1] III, pp. 763–803; *The Past Recaptured*: pp. 51–82 (RH); pp. 85–140 (C&W).

[2] III, p. 872; *The Past Recaptured*: p. 133 (RH); p. 230 (C&W).

in Paris or at Balbec, Brichot's look behind his glasses or the puns of Professor Cottard.

Generally speaking, the theme of the two kinds of memory, which constitutes the basic philosophical thesis of the work, seems to me to be far and away one of the least original. To begin with, the idea was not of course a new one when Proust took it up again. It was not only not new, but about 1910 it dominated the scene in the form of a fashionable commonplace introduced by Bergson. Before Bergson, it had been the basic theme of George Eliot's novels. Proust, as we know, read and liked them very much. We also come across the same idea, treated with incomparable power by a writer whom nobody knew at the time: Kierkegaard, who distinguishes in his Introduction to *The Banquet* (*In vino veritas*) between what he calls recollection (*souvenir*) and what he calls memory (*mémoire*). The curious thing is that he endows his memory with the suddenness and spontaneity recognised by Proust as "true" memory, but unlike Proust it is to reflective recollection, to the *art* of remembering, that Kierkegaard attributes creative power—the faculty, for example, of systematically experiencing homesickness by means of "recollection" while remaining at home. At the time when he wrote, Kierkegaard was original whereas at the time when Proust wrote he came not only after Bergson, but after all the discussions by psychologists about "affective memory." In the belief that he has reached the timeless, the imperishable, Proust only gets as far as Théodule Ribot's heels. He betrays his latent materialism, or his associationist empiricism, by making the release of "true memory" dependent on a *sensation*, the recollection based on identity, coincidence between present and past sensations and as a result, on some external factor which is always fortuitous. With Bergsonian spiritualism there is never anything external; it is the intuition of the "depths of the self" in its pure inwardness which alone can procure such an experience. Proust's psychology combines a little spiritualism with a little associationist sensualism. He becomes more Bergsonian as he becomes more of a theorist, as we can see, for example, from his views on artistic creation. He moves towards sensualism and associationism when he describes, without becoming too exalted, what is going on inside him and when the narrator of the real becomes the speaker again. But whatever the philosophy he works out in this context, or the experience he describes, the superposing of a past and a present sensation to which everything suddenly clings must certainly have been very strong for him—so strong that he probably thought it natural and easy to communicate its charm. The charm of this contact between ourselves and our past is a fact that cannot be contested and has been experienced by us. Yet if everyone experiences it on his own account, is it not just as difficult to make a third person share it as it is to make him share the experience of passionate love?

I must admit this much: the passages that I like least in Proust, the ones that I re-read with the least interest, are precisely these resurrections which emerge from his "second memory"—beginning with the story of the *madeleine*, which always reminds me of a piece of schoolboy "narration": "*Tout Combray . . . est sorti de ma tasse de thé* (The whole of Combray . . . sprang from my cup of tea),"[1] which is weak as a closing sentence; those evocations of impressions suggested by place names, domestic habits, changes of season; those disillusioned discoveries of familiar places which have shrunk and become unrecognisable when one returns to them after a long absence; those amalgams of a name and an image, of a feeling and a circumstance, of the sound of a heating installation and a period of one's life, of a smell and the memory of a great love.

Yes, all that is true; it all happens to us, but we have to admit that it does not possess much interest except for ourselves. Apart from the fact that it was something which happened to *him*, it is sometimes impossible to understand why Proust dwells at such length on certain things. Let me make myself clear: it is the thing that bores me and not the length. For if what is known as brevity means never writing anything unless it contains a new idea, Proust's style is, generally speaking, one of the most rapid that exists, except precisely in those passages which he himself believed to be the most lyrical. His psychology which, as it

[1] I, p. 48; *Swann's Way:* I, p. 36 (RH); , p.I 62 (C&W).

happens, is completely associationist, turns against him here; for if it is true, as he alleges, that these affective constructions are due exclusively to fortuitous meetings between a sensation and a feeling, they are evidently without any sort of resonance save for the person in whom they take place. We have our own, which belong to us alone, and it is not the fact in general which matters, but the personal content which is only moving to the person who experiences it.

My reservations are not dictated by a desire to condemn for the ten-thousandth time associationism, which appears to be an outmoded psychology. Whatever the psychological theory into which they will be fitted, the affective phenomena described by Proust are before everything else things which have been lived through, and it is as such and in his capacity as a novelist that very fortunately he describes them. But it follows that it is the novelist who must be criticised for not having seen to what a limited extent such feelings are capable of being shared. I am thinking, for example, of all the pages with names of places. Everything that a name can evoke for each of us by its sonority alone is as far from being obligatory for other people as the states in which we are placed by the sight of colors. The knowledge that a friend is plunged into convulsions at the sight of violet, even if it is a very intense experience for him, could do no more than leave us with a mild feeling of boredom. I often skip a good many pages when I feel that one of those Proustian boats is about to arrive, drifting among the waves of "involuntary memory." And yet it is to this memory that he continually attributed the source and the novelty of his work. We should, however, observe that he does not make it intervene deliberately, that he only thinks about it when he turns his eyes on himself and evokes not an event, but a feeling which detaches him from the event as he had already detached himself from it at the very moment it happened. We have to ask ourselves if Proust's literary health, which he always believed was dependent on a return into himself, was not in fact due to those moments when he forgot himself, when he was no longer, while facing the virgin screen, anything but the simultaneous spectator and director of the film.

For nobody has been able to speak as brilliantly of mankind except Montaigne. Nobody has been so energetic in bringing them on to the stage; nobody has pinned down in the way that he has everything that escapes us each day because we are incapable of recounting it; nobody has proved a winner with such regularity except perhaps Saint-Simon. But though by no means such a fanatical visionary of the real as Saint-Simon, Proust excels him by the knowledge he acquires of it. His sensibility is subtler, more varied, more generous than his with the result that he attains the moral truths that Saint-Simon, whose marvelous retinal frenzy appeals in vain to the obtuse mind, lacks on account of his exasperation.

IN ANY CASE, Proust is in no sense an analytical novelist. A novel is analytical when analysis replaces or even creates the event. Now Proustian analysis is always a reflection on events *which have taken place*. In *Remembrance of Things Past* the parts devoted without cuts to the narration of events, descriptions, reports of conversations, can easily be separated from the comments on them, and more easily still from the thoughts on life in general which may emerge. At present Proust is given credit retrospectively for a formal revolution of the novel (an expression which probably means revolutionising the form of the novel). To tell the truth, I find it difficult to see in what it is supposed to consist. I should be more inclined myself to give Proust credit for something much rarer: revolutionising the material of literature. Twenty or thirty years ago he was actually criticised for doing precisely the opposite: for not inventing a new form which was adapted to the treasures he put into the content. He was an aesthete, a European man of letters, a mandarin who had remained faithful to classical form; he had not dared to carry through his revolution to the end; his literary suicide was no more than a suicide "at high interest," wrote Sartre, who set up in opposition to him Faulkner and the American novelists as examples of classic writers.[1]

Today when the technical prowess of the Americans has lost

[1] *Situations*, I, p. 77.

its power of gripping us, has it not become almost obvious that novels written in the style of a Faulkner or a Hemingway are much more a matter of arrangement, more "literary", more aesthetic than the Proustian novel? These novels will in future have a place in literary history; they represent a "moment" in the history of the novel—the moment of reaction against the analytical novel. But Proust did not care a straw about the history of the genre. Why should he suppress through bias those long meditations, half-organised and promptly disorganised, those hesitations, interpretations, interior repetitions which in fact are always with us and which follow, for example, the departure or death of someone we love? And why should one give them the entirely literary form of the "inner monologue," when it is clear that in reality they do not assume this form, that they are often passably elaborated and well expressed, and that it is untrue, or very rarely, that we think in a telegraphic style? Whether his book is a novel based on memories or memoirs full of facts which were imagined or treated in the manner of a novelist, why should he deprive himself of the right to re-examine the things that had happened to him and to tell us at length what he thinks of them from the moment at which the thing begins to *happen*? The behaviorist novel is a literary artifice in the same way as a novel which sets out to be purely interior. As Sartre himself has admirably demonstrated, both are works of art, stylizations of reality: in other words, lies.[1] We do not live solely by means of our gestures or our thoughts or merely in face of the events and the sights which are presented to us. In spite of his desire to create a work of art, Proust seems to have preferred truth to art. By never speaking except in his own name and by never making anything but legitimate suppositions about the interior life of other people, he has shown the perpetual and inextricable mixing of the inner and outer life, that is to say, the impossibility—I am speaking in terms of exactness and not of the aesthetic or the poetic—of separating them from one another. The coexistence of the most diverse spheres is a rule for him, as it is in life. Proust does not choose: he relates.

[1] *Situations*, I, in the essay on "François Mauriac et la liberté."

One of the principal characteristics of the analytical novel, as of the novels of Faulkner and Hemingway, which are the antithesis of it, is its uniformity of style so that events and characters only exist, in both cases, by virtue of an artistic tension, by their translation into a given form. With Proust, on the contrary, every character speaks in his own particular manner. There is the language of Bloch, of M. de Norpois, of Swann, of Brichot, of Cottard, of Mme Verdurin, Saniette, Françoise, Aimé, Jupien, Legrandin, Gilberte, Odette, etc., which are as different from one another as they are from the language of Proust. It is not simply a question of the idea often put forward by critics in relation to great novelists and great dramatists—that they possess the talent to make their characters "independent of their creator" and to make them live on their own account in our imagination. With Proust it is not simply a question of that. It is not only possible to make Charlus, Norpois, Cottard, Morel and Swann move and speak in our imagination: it is even more surprising to see the extent to which they differ from one another in the smallest details. They are independent of their scenario-writer and their audience; they are also independent *of one another*, not simply as a result of the differences in their respective biographies, but in themselves. In Balzac the characters are all differentiated by means of their stories, but they all bear that same stamp. In Proust no story is really the distinguishing mark of this or that character: their stories could all be alike, but the characters would not differ any the less among themselves, in themselves and by the stuff of which they are made. All Balzac's characters talk Balzac; one cannot regard the vulgar typographical patois of a Nucingen or a Gobseck as an original language. In Molière, Harpagon and M. Jourdain each has his own unique personality, but five lines of any replies from either of them are before all else five lines by Molière. With Proust it is not only a vocabulary, a syntax, a system of metaphors, a diction which are invented or completely reconstructed; it is a manner of thinking, feeling, a way of being. Let us suppose that the whole of *Remembrance of Things Past* came to be destroyed and that only twenty phrases of Bloch's, twenty of Norpois's, twenty of Aimé's,

etc. had survived—one would hardly suspect that they had all
come from the same pen. It is not only hundreds of expressions
and turns of speech proper to each of his characters that Proust
finds; it is also what the people say—the content of their thought
which is very much their own. With a certain amount of apti-
tude, we can easily imitate people's manner of speaking and
behavior, but if we try to put what we see or hear down on
paper, we are soon brought to a halt because we lack the raw
material which they alone can provide, that is to say, their ideas.
Proust manages to make every character speak and act in his own
style, but each time about a different subject and in different
circumstances, so that, as in Italian Comedy, each remains true
to his own type: while improvising himself and "surprising" us
by surpassing himself, he confirms the image of himself. In
Remembrance of Things Past we not only see the exceptionally
gifted pasticher at work, because by doing a pastiche we imitate
what an author has already said, in the same way that we parody
a friend in circumstances in which we have already seen him.
But it is a rare thing to be able to construct in his entirety a
character who thinks, speaks and behaves differently from our-
selves and who nevertheless does not bear the trade mark of the
author as obviously as the heroes of Balzac or Molière. The
character really becomes the sort of palpably unexpected being
whom we normally only come across in everyday life and not in
literature because such an unexpected person is not due to an
exaltation of imagination, but to calming it down, thanks to
something which comes from outside and which occupies him
without tension on his part; plunging us in this way into a
fountain of youthfulness, producing something that is so rarely
available—a total absence of boredom lasting for several hours.
When we know people well, what interests us passionately is
what happens to them each day. With Proust we burn with
desire to "know" what happened to so-and-so on such-and-such
an evening. When we go out with him, we know that we are
going to find "something different."

Proust is first and foremost this: the inexhaustible presenter of
what is completely external, what comes from outside. We have

not always noticed it precisely because what is external presents itself to us, with him as in life, all wrapped up in reflections, appreciations and considerations, whereas the "modern" novel has accustomed us to a false exterior which consists of relating subjective and semi-oneiric data in newspaper language.

PROUST'S TASTE FOR THE REAL in all its details explains why *Remembrance of Things Past* divides up into huge fragments. If he needs several hundred pages in order to describe a soirée, it is because he lives through every instant and every aspect of it from the time of arrival to the time of departure. It has been said that the Proustian novel is a continuity. It is a strange thing that for forty years people have been repeating the same phrases about the experience of time being turned upside down in Proust, about the continuity of Proustian time, the importance of the passage of time in Proust's work, as a result, it must be admitted, of one's faith in the philosophical affirmations of the author himself, when in fact it is sufficient to read *Remembrance of Things Past*, to see it as a novel and not merely as a series of demonstrations made palatable by "concrete" examples, in order to perceive that, leaving aside some theoretical hors-d'oeuvre and some declarations of principle, which anyway are rather hollow, time does not play any part in the story, in the *unfolding* of the story. Or, more exactly, there is no unfolding of the story, not the least sign of continuous progression, never the faintest sense of the passing of time. We are always in the present. The narrator lives from day to day. In fact, *Remembrance of Things Past* is a juxtaposition of half-days and soirées, a number of which are separated from one another by periods of several years. The narrator devotes fewer pages to describing ten of these years than he does to describing a single lunch in the dining-room of the Grand Hotel at Balbec. Here again, with his philosophy of memory, Proust embroiders a little on his work by adding to his story a philosophy of Time. While in Balzac, Tolstoy and Zola, we witness effective changes taking place day by day or hour by hour; while a month, a week, a day may be decisive for Rubempré, Birotteau, or Rastignac, Proust by comparison is the painter of immobility. He is only himself when he forgets Time, when he *is* simply in Mme de Villeparisis's salon or in a restaurant where he is dining on a foggy evening with Saint-Loup. We never see the characters in the process of changing: we suddenly find that they have changed. They bring off staggering "come backs." If something emerges from *Remembrance of Things Past*, it is that we are never directly conscious of time.

We know the extent to which Proust was impressed by the Balzacian idea of making certain characters reappear from one novel to another. He has told us (one might say almost "sung") of the joy that Balzac must have felt the day he realized that several novels published by him could be linked to one another. In an essay on Balzac dealing with the famous meeting (in *Les Illusions perdues*) between Carlos Herrera and Rubempré in the road early in the morning in front of the ruins of the Château de Rastignac, Proust speaks of the "ray of light emerging from the depths of the work" which fell on the two or rather the three characters because Rastignac is invisibly present.[1] But the characters with multiple appearances do not perform the same function in Balzac and Proust. The Balzacian novel is activist. (This is obvious in the case of the Balzacian novel itself because it is an adventure story. But it is also true of most of the great nineteenth-century novels where the events which transform the situations have an absolute bearing on the fate of the characters.) In Proust, on the other hand, there is no fundamental change in M. de Charlus's position when, having fallen in love with Morel, he frequents Mme Verdurin's salon—the salon where it would previously have been inconceivable for him to show his "august toes." This "smart" affair does not exactly bring anything new except that it throws further light on a character. It is a projector; it is not an effective transformation. Proust very often repeats that in fashionable society life nothing ever happens. (Sainte-Beuve, he said, employs the treasures of subtlety in order

[1] *By Way of Sainte-Beuve*, translated and edited by Sylvia Townsend Warner, 1958.
I have retained the French title, *Contre Sainte-Beuve*, in the text because it reflects more accurately Proust's attitude towards Sainte Beuve. *Tr.*

to analyse the differences in atmosphere and psychology of the various literary salons without managing to make us aware of the slightest difference between them and in this way demonstrates, without realising what he is doing, one thing only: *"le néant,"* the emptiness of salon life.) The only changes which really affect people in Proust are the indirect changes which are the result of the war: the casualties, the losses of fortune, notwithstanding the fact that life, from the point of view of those who live it, preserves, so to speak, a static content which is often tabulated at the outset. There again, what a strange lack of feeling for the evolution of human beings and the unpredictable richness of the future on the part of our supposedly great novelist of temporality! Although in English novelists like George Eliot and Thomas Hardy, whom Proust admired, we are conscious in chapter after chapter of the slow, steady passage of what might be called biographical time, and though in Flaubert we feel beneath the seemingly monotonous regularity of everyday life the continual slipping away of the ground which undermines the very foundations of existence, the narrator of *Remembrance of Things Past* presents us with a succession of portraits of his characters whom he happens to meet after an interval of ten or twenty years. Every time he is considerably "surprised" to find that their faces and situations are no longer quite the same as they were the first time he found his way into a particular salon thirty years ago. He himself is only indirectly aware that he has aged when at an age that one suspects is verging on forty he makes people laugh by saying to Gilberte de Saint-Loup who has just suggested dinner alone together: *"Si vous ne trouvez pas compromettant de venir diner seule avec un jeune homme.* (If you don't find it compromising to dine alone with a young man)."[1] A psychoanalyst would probably call it a childhood fixation . . . The narrator asserts by implication: "I find it incomprehensible that I should be forty; it's unreal." He is amazed, as though faced with an extraordinary series of metamorphoses, by the most smoothly normal and predictable changes which have taken place in other people and remains "surprised" in their presence, imitating the

[1] III, p. 931; *The Past Recaptured*: p. 180 (RH); p. 312 (C&W).

public and the newspapers who every year are "surprised" by
the return of periods of great cold or intense heat, as though it
were a question of unnatural cataclysms which somehow justified
the inadequacy of the supplies of coal and ice. Emmanuel Berl
observes in *Sylvia* that the old men in *Remembrance of Things Past*
never really look like old men: they are young people made up
to look like old men. They caricature themselves. Bloch becomes
"like a father." One is either an old man or one is not—the
narrator's grandfather is one because he is an old man at the
beginning of the novel—but if a person is not an old man to
start with, he can never become one. Old age, however, does
make its appearance by a series of jolts and is felt to be irrational,
unjustified; in a word, unjust. It is a curious thing, but this
attachment to a childhood never does any harm in Proust to the
extreme maturity of thought and does not prevent a radical
elimination of the psychological naïveté of adolescence when it
is a matter of explaining feelings and actions. Nevertheless,
Proust (unlike Montaigne) did not possess the art or the
strength to reconcile himself to the idea that time passes and that
we grow old. The day he accepts the position is also the day
when he becomes reconciled not to growing old, but to dying. In
the meantime it is always at one of those moments when time
seems to come to a stop and we discover that we have "grown old,"
that time "has passed," that everything "has greatly changed,"
that Saint-Loup "has broken" with Rachel, and on the same
occasion that he "no longer cares for literature" and "is no
longer" a Dreyfusard. The reason for the reappearance of a
character is usually therefore to demolish a legend rather than to
provoke a resurgence of the action. There is no action. Proust's
characters as a whole are something like a *corps de ballet* "which is
always starting up again." They do not confine themselves to
reappearances in different lights; they unite. They end by form-
ing nothing more than a single inextricable group. Swann's
way and Guermantes' way cannot remain separated; not only
has Swann always known the Guermantes, but Saint-Loup
marries Gilberte who was Proust's great love while Saint-Loup
was his best friend; but Odette, who was "the lady in pink", a

demi-mondaine of whom we caught a glimpse at the home of the narrator's uncle, before becoming Mme Swann, ends by being the Duc de Guermantes' last great love. Not only does Saint-Loup become a homosexual, but the young man for whom he falls turns out to be none other than Morel, once the unhappy great love of his uncle Charlus, a former passing fancy of his other uncle, Sosthène, and the nephew of the famous valet of Proust's own uncle. Mme Verdurin becomes the Princesse de Guermantes. Jupien is transformed into the male nurse of Charlus's senility after being first his seducer, then his procurer. In the course of the last general meeting of the shareholders in the society of *Remembrance of Things Past*—the one where the guests give the impression of "looking glum"—everybody is there including Rachel. Those who are not there (Cottard, Bergotte, Saint-Loup, Saniette) would have been there if they had not been dead: it is the final meeting which kills Berma when she learns that her daughter and son-in-law have come to "suck up" to Rachel in order that they may be received. Everything mixes and collapses in a horrifying mixture: one no longer knows where the Prince de Guermantes' leg is, Odette de Forcheville's arm, and whether by pulling Bloch's beard one is going to make M. de Bréauté-Consalvi's monocle fall.

IN THIS WAY Proust's characters change without changing. Sometimes they undergo a complete change without anything remarkable happening to them. On the other hand, there are times when their existence undergoes a major transformation without their changing. Finally, we might always say of each of them, as happens to us in life, that "he has greatly changed" and that he is "always just the same." Indeed, beside the unchangingness of a M. de Norpois we find the inexplicable mutation of Saint-Loup. But, to tell the truth, the mutation is only apparent: Saint-Loup was always exactly what the narrator sees him to be and what a head waiter, Aimé, tells him that he is, but up to that time we had not seen him in this light. The change therefore takes place primarily by means of information received. If,

however, certain people change in themselves, it is only because
time accentuates certain tendencies which are already present in
them, throws into relief some traits and attenuates others. Thus
it is in spite of and within the limits of their unchanging charac-
ter and destiny that the Proustian characters undergo a process
of renewal. The head waiter is always the same head waiter; I
shall come across him tomorrow in the same place, but he will
renew himself because his mimicry will be even more fetching
than it was yesterday, as one says of a singer that he "renews
himself" while remaining faithful to his chosen line. In their
constancy, the characters of the Proustian comedy are nevethe-
less unpredictable, such is the way in which once more the even-
ing dinner is going to change them in themselves. That is why
the most important changes in the lives of the people erupt with a
meteoric and incomprehensible suddenness; that is why the least
important happenings ("Bloch is received by the Princesse de
Guermantes") appear considerable simply because they are
effective and modify concrete situations. Moreover, Proust
enjoys showing us personal renewals, which are not merely
changes in social status (there are few of them or they only
happen to secondary characters) as though they had no roots in
the past and are therefore not the result of a process of evolution,
but the equivalent of the birth of a fresh individual. He an-
nounces them carelessly, on the side, so repugnant does he find
it to imagine progressive change. There is Octave, whose nick-
name is "I am in the soup," the idiotic young spark in *Within a
Budding Grove*, who becomes in *The Past Recaptured* an able writer
whose latest work, which the narrator never stops thinking about,
has just turned modern literature upside down! Nothing which
takes place between the two appearances of Octave enables us to
link them. Proustian time is not creative. Its role, while bringing
about changes in the social situation—minimal changes which
nevertheless seem of capital importance to the interested parties
and are always announced with surprise by the narrator—is to
reveal the true nature of the characters, to unveil what men
already were without out knowing it. The Albertine of whom we
catch a glimpse on the beach is already everything which will be

discovered by the narrator as a result of his posthumous investigation of her liaisons.

It is curious to observe that Proustian narration is completely lacking in temporal realism. Proust is essentially a realist in the present, in description, in production, in impression, but he ceases to be a realist when it comes to the linking together of the different moments. In his case, intemporality is sometimes pushed to the point where it makes the events related impossible in practice. Thus the escapade of Rachel and Saint-Loup—already very long, which begins in the country, continues in the restaurant, and ends in a private room—takes place on the same day as the famous afternoon party at Mme de Villeparisis's which itself would be sufficient to fill up several weeks. Proust's insensitiveness to time is also apparent in minor matters: the famous article sent to *Le Figaro* when the author is a very young man is published towards the end of *The Captive*, that is to say, something like fifteen years after being sent. In the meantime Proust has opened *Le Figaro* every morning to see whether his article is there. The Proustian narration is as intemporal as the unity of time in classic tragedy and comedy and like them implies unity of place or places (in very small numbers) and the so-called unity of action, meaning that all the characters know or end by knowing one another. We have already seen that the members of Proust's cast find themselves together in the same salon in *The Past Recaptured*. Each of them exercises, or has exercised, in one way or another, an influence on the life of all the others. From the very start of the book the way is prepared for this general meeting. Like Mme Verdurin, the narrator wants to have the whole of his world at hand. This explains a number of improbabilities which are of no importance and which we do not even notice at a first reading because in the Proustian novel it is not a matter of action, but of pictures: the dubious hotel which the narrator enters by chance turns out to be under the management of Jupien and it so happens that his visit take place on the evening that Baron de Charlus goes there to have himself tortured. Elsewhere it is Aimé, the head waiter at the Grand Hotel at Balbec, who happens to be the head waiter at the Paris restaurant where Rachel and Saint-Loup go to lunch in the company of the narrator—the lunch during which M. de Charlus sends for Aimé to come and speak to him at the door of his carriage which has stopped in front of the restaurant in a place which enables Saint-Loup to recognise him by catching sight of him through the window. Proust's coincidences tend to congeal the characters and to level out time. On the one hand, if it is necessary for somebody to get married, Proust will choose a wife for him from among the known people (Saint-Loup marrying Gilberte; Octave, known as "in the soup," marrying Andrée). On the other hand, when it is necessary for something fresh to happen, the events are crammed into a few lines so that he can pass on as quickly as possible to what really interests him: a static moment, a soirée, a dinner. He then proceeds simultaneously with the telescoping of time and the fantastic multiplication of the threads attaching the characters to one another. In *Cities of the Plain*, for example, M. de Charlus catches sight of Morel (whom he does not know) in military uniform, at a station, which turns out to be Doncières, a town already well known to the reader, where by a piece of luck Morel is doing his military service. At the same moment the narrator goes through the station; M. de Charlus sends him to find (meaning to accost on his behalf) Morel who turns out to be the nephew of the valet of Proust's uncle (but M. de Charlus does not know that). Morel is a violinist and the same evening, pretending that he is an elderly relative of Morel's, M. de Charlus turns up at a villa where the violinist happens to be playing on this particular day. The people are none other than the Verdurins (whom M. de Charlus obviously doesn't know) and it turns out that Proust (who knows the baron very well) has also been invited to the soirée!

But this soirée, once all the characters are well and truly enclosed behind the lighted windows of the great La Raspelière salon to which they have been brought high-handedly and *manu militari*, this soirée where the narrator is sure that nothing more is going to happen and where everybody, without budging, can be himself, is his real subject—outside time.

PROUST SUBSCRIBED to a fairly simple conception of "literary creation". He believed that every artist "carries" inside him a world of primitive images which precedes experience and is independent of it: a secret "country", as he said of Barbey d'Aurevilly. He does not see that for him, Proust, this world is only a rebound in the direction of the exterior of what the "artist" had first of all discovered outside himself and has in the main drawn from observation. At the beginning of the preface to *Contre Sainte-Beuve*, we find this sentence which appears strange coming from his pen: "*Chaque jour j'attache moins de prix à l'intelligence* (Every day I attach less importance to intelligence)." He does not appear to have any inkling that the idea of intelligence to which he is referring—the intelligence which divides, cheapens, only grasps the "externals" of reality—is no more than a conception which became fashionable in his own time: the time of Bergson and the "anti-intellectualist" reaction which was going on all over Europe. It is this intelligence, in the special sense given to it here and not the literal sense of the act of understanding, which would prove fatal to judgement of taste. His theory of literary "creation" is linked to his theory of "true memory" which was another product of contemporary fashion. To be sure, Proust gave Sainte-Beuve retrospectively the most well-deserved and the most amusing rebuke possible. But if it is true to say that Sainte-Beuve preferred Vicq d'Azyr to Stendhal, one is sorry to have to point out that Proust himself regarded Maeterlinck, the Comtesse de Noailles, and Léon Daudet as geniuses, and not Max Jacob, Apollinaire, or Jarry. Some people, with the intention of excusing Proust, maintain that his literary judgements can be explained on the grounds of friendship. It is useless to emphasise the fact that this pretended excuse makes the position even worse because besides being a writer who regarded the work of art as sacred, completely separate from everyday life and relationships, the judgements in question are incorporated in *Remembrance of Things Past* itself. We should also recall that Proust only saw the Comtesse de Noailles once or twice in his life (as Emmanuel Berl has shown in *Présence des morts*). It was therefore without indulgence that he judged her

to be the greatest French poet of his time. And in a different
context we may feel irritated by the salon-like way in which he
uses the names of great painters, incapable as he is of seeing a
handsome face without speaking of Mantegna or Carpaccio and
comparing Mme de Putbus's lady's maid to a Giorgione. What is
more, the hint of a joke and a useful sense of erotic analogy are
mixed up in the last comparison. But it is with seriousness and
respect that Proust writes: "*Il [Swann] aimait encore, en effet, voir en
sa femme un Botticelli* (He still liked to see a Botticelli in his wife)."
These weaknesses come, alas, straight from the "world of images"
that "every great artist" carries inside himself.

For, in the last analysis, is not the permanent character of the
great truths that a Proust or a Montaigne make known to us a
matter of being able to do without images when the greater part
of our supposed theoretical truths are no more than images which
for a moment freshen up our vision of the real before becoming
used up? Proust touches on the supreme truths when he describes
exactly what happens.

In an article on intentionality, Sartre said that "we are
delivered from Proust" because we now know, thanks to Husserl,
that "if we are fond of a person it is because the person is
amiable." In spite of the innumerable proofs to the contrary
inflicted on us by life, I am not going to haggle over the question
itself. What is piquant about Sartre's words is the way in which
he plays on the double meaning of the adjective "*aimable*"; the
basic and the current sense. In the first sense of "worthy to be
loved," it is a question of an old and dubious thesis; in the
second sense of "whom one loves, who pleases," it is a case of a
self-evident truth or an observation of fact. But above all
intentionality itself is really only an image.[1] Proust's "interiorist"
metaphors, to be sure, are only metaphors: but fortunately they
are accessories because we cannot afford to neglect metaphors,
given the fact that Proust has told us in the first place how every-
thing went off effectively, that he followed the thread of events.

No doubt these events, in their pure state, strike him to such

[1] *Situations*, I, p. 34: "Une Idée fondamentale de Husserl: L'intention-
nalité."

an extent that he who is so quick to reassemble all his characters in the same room, as though there were only one dining-room in the whole world, the dining-room in the Grand Hotel at Balbec, is naïvely astonished, on the other hand, when it is a question of love, by the apparent coincidences, the "chances" that turn up in life. If Swann had not known his grandfather, if Swann had not been an amateur of art, if he had not talked to him about the church at Balbec, if he had not said that this church might have been in Persia, if a company had not decided at the same moment to build a comfortable hotel at Balbec, he would not have met Albertine and Albertine would not, perhaps, have been killed in an accident with a horse.

These coincidences, which seem always to have favored the birth of feelings, are always apparent precisely because those feelings had not yet come into being at that time. Chances are not like that: they are simple facts. Something has to happen and everything happens like that. We can only stay at a particular hotel if somebody has given us the address. Proust was not wrong in thinking—but he was wrong in finding it surprising—that, if Mme de Stermaria had not cancelled the engagement the evening that she was to have dined with him on the island in the Bois de Boulogne, she would perhaps have played the part in his life that in the event was played by Albertine. But the narrator's astonishment, which was the legitimate fruit of the backward glances of a man who measures the striking disproportion between the feeble beginnings of a passion and what follows, between the moment when the events leading up to it are not yet distinguishable from other everyday happenings and the sudden upward surge which with a totally unexpected force tears them away from everyday life, makes us live on two levels at the same time. Our astonishment is an episode *in the novel*; it is not a *theory* about the contingency of the birth of love. For the rest, there is no need to read Proust in order to hold theories of love. Nobody is without them, alas! But on the other hand, what we cannot find out by ourselves is the truth of he details.

THIS CONCERN FOR accuracy of detail often makes people say

of Proust, as of Montaigne, that he is a superficial or fashionable writer. "Fashionable" is a reproach which must have made Proust smile—Proust who had demonstrated the idiocy, the grossness and the boredom not only of the fashionable society life of his time, but of all fashionable society life, and had done it so effectively that after reading him we lose in retrospect all confidence in the real atmosphere which must have reigned, for example, in the most "brilliant" salons of the eighteenth century, and we become aware of the fact that "society" has never been and cannot be anything but a myth. Proust was not of course without his weaknesses. When the ladies at the Duchesse de Guermantes' move in front of the Princesse de Parme in order to go down on their knees, as one should in the presence of royalty, she raises them to their feet, pretends to be surprised, strokes their cheeks and embraces them. And Proust comments more or less in these terms: I wonder how politeness could exist in an egalitarian society, since the absence of respect to be paid to a superior would prevent such exquisite politeness as that shown by the Princesse de Parme.

Is it a piece of mockery? For how can one speak of *politeness* in relation to a ceremonial which is so empty and so devoid of meaning, a series of antics which are so painful because we know perfectly well that they do not correspond to any "superiority," any "duty," any "gentility" which really exist, and that in this instance the "bounty" of the supposedly superior person is no more than a way of feeling, and making others feel, her supposed superiority? Does not politeness, which is simply the way of handling other people that we impose on ourselves even if the other person is not a friend—or, for that matter, even if he is— does it not need, in order to mean anything, the equality of individuals? And, as Proust shows very clearly everywhere else, true politeness only exists when it is voluntary.

But there are people who regard Proust as a society author in a different sense, that is to say, not simply because he displays a complacent attitude towards society, but because he deals with life and not the meaning of life; with the surface and not the depths; with the appearances and not the roots of man or with

what goes beyond man. Some people regard a writer as pro-
found if he works out a metaphysical theory as economically as
possible. Does not the accumulation of material details with-
out ever summing them up in a general proposition which holds
good, without ever ceasing to add an observation to a story or a
story to an observation and without attempting or even per-
mitting a synthesis, but neglecting the summing-up and the
interpretation in order to run after some fresh detail which never
fails to postpone both—does not all this show a lack of intellec-
tual curiosity and is it not a sign of looking indulgently on the
vain glitter of desultory remarks in the superficial mix-up of the
harrassing and unpredictable diversity of human nature? It is
an odd thing, but people often see Proust as a profound writer
in precisely those areas in which he is not profound—in his
theory of time and memory, and as a superficial chronicler
when he describes with a tireless simplicity those marvelous
details which he alone has been able to bring out.

Proust is not simply one of the greatest comic geniuses who
have ever existed; he is also one of the most serious men who
have ever lived. In *The Guermantes Way* he defines the precise
nature of the superiority of the great pianist over the mediocre
pianist. There is a tendency to imagine that one is better at
interpreting a sonata than the other. On the contrary, he does
not, even in a masterly fashion, *interpret* the sonata; he ceases to
exist in front of it and by his intermediary the sonata speaks for
itself. That is what sometimes happens to Proust himself in the
face of reality.

It is often said that Proust is the pure psychologist and lacks
any metaphysical underside. But is not "making" metaphysics
out of something experienced a sign that it is already becoming a
matter of indifference to us? Proust is too passionate a being
ever to detach himself from what really happens inside him.
Only time, even for him, can bring about this form of loosening.
When it happens, it is not a "metaphysical dimension" which
has "come into being," but another experience of life which
supervenes. A metaphysic, when transformed into a supposedly
direct experience, is nothing but an attempt to "force" things a

little, to make the story of oneself, which underlies all existence, sound "interesting"; and it is done in order to escape the merciless "progression" of life. On the contrary, the richest experiences, those which we have lived through and understood, and which alone enable us to make progress in our knowledge of ourselves and other people, can only leave in the mind—as it is said long after the flight and death of the Fugitive—*"une impression où la tristesse est encore dominée par la fatigue* (An impression in which sadness is still dominated by weariness)." Any other impression would mean that we had added, artificially, an element of mystery, that we had plunged ahead of ourselves, that we had anticipated some future or inaccessible role, interpreted our present way of life in order to provide ourselves with a little distraction, and we should no longer be talking about something we really understood. But the effective comprehension, when we eventually attain it, becomes so much our own evidence, coincides so exactly with ourselves that in fact it can only appear banal and once again leaves us alone with ourselves.

Nothing which is really ours is uplifting or elevating or metaphysical: these are expressions whose outsides are used by us. We only have an alleged "revelation" of reality when we have no permanent contact with it. It is then that *"nous sommes attirés par toute vie qui nous représente quelque chose d'inconnu, par une dernière illusion à détruire* (we are attracted by every form of life which represents to us something unknown and strange, by a last illusion still unshattered)".[1] Why illusion? Not that the life we discover should necessarily be uninteresting. The illusion consists rather in this: that the life we are seeking to approach, to understand or to live ourselves, could continue not to be ours even though we have lived it, could retain the attraction and the mystery which belong to anything that is alien to us while at the same time becoming our daily life. Inversely, the metaphysical lie consists in pretending that an existence which is nevertheless undoubtedly our own remains partly unknown, by lending it the engaging mystery of the life of a character whom we are pretending that we only know from afar, as we can do, even in spite

[1] II, p. 567; *The Guermantes Way*: I, p. 1120 (RH); VI, p. 354 (C&W).

of ourselves, when we speak about ourselves and make a confession about our life to another person, less for the purpose of
informing him about it than to attract him.

But if he avoids metaphysics by means of exaltation, Proust
does not attempt either to obtain a metaphysical effect by means
of depression, by an exaggerated stylization of the appalling
insignificance of life, as Flaubert so often did. For once again
everything would be too transparent and the way of truth far
too easily indicated if we were all "simple hearts" or Bouvards
and Pécuchets. The desire to describe men's experience while
purging it of all the knowledge that we have of it, which is sometimes *true* (that is where the difficulty lies), is just as artificial, in
spite of the fact that Flaubert extracts from it a poetical side
that is shattering, as to imagine a man with the features of a
Dostoyevsky hero driven out of his mind by the sacred. Proust
has no taste for inventions, fakes, unjustified leaps and misleading invocations. He never establishes relations between two
things which have none. I know of no finer meditation on
absence, death and oblivion than *The Sweet Cheat Gone*: nothing
more transparent, patient, supple, sincere and a more careful
statement of genuine effects. If it existed, that would be metaphysics: that deepening of real life, that absence of sham, of
complacency; that modesty, that calm manner of presenting
oneself full face to a certain number of illuminations, where there
is a sense of the meaning of life—things which fall to us of their
own accord and our only course is not to run away from them.
Proust does not belong to the category of overheated fifty-year-
olds, eleventh-hour adolescents who by a monumental piece of
stupidity suddenly nullify all the interesting things they have
said previously. We can feel sure that he at all events is not
suddenly going to take up yogi, "to weep and believe," fall in
love with Zen Buddhism, generalized relativity, Heraclitus,
adhere to the Golden Section, wave mechanism or Moral
Rearmament. He keeps hysteria in reserve for the domain in
which it has its place—everyday life and love relations—but
banishes it from his work where he becomes the sanest of men.
Remembrance of Things Past, even in its weaknesses, is one of those

rare books which provide us with an example of completely adult thought.

In his psychology of everyday life, or rather let us say, his understanding of human nature and in his interpretation of its actions, Proust seems sometimes to be satisfied with explanations which are either too facile or too complicated. It may be due to the fact that all his characters are idle. In the next chapter we shall try to discover the function of their idleness. The static, timeless nature of *Remembrance of Things Past* is reinforced by the fact that it is peopled by a crowd of characters who never work at anything. The only people who are ever seen at work are domestic servants and expensive doctors. The third category of active people who play a part is of course the category of the great creators. But given the Proustian conception of literary or artistic creation, we never actually see them at work and by definition we cannot do so. Elstir provides an exception on the afternoon that the narrator watches the painter working on his canvas. Again, it is an Elstir who has "arrived," whose goal has already been reached, who is applying his discoveries and whose talent will not renew itself. Bergotte only shows himself as a man of the world; Vinteuil as the timorous and persecuted lower middle-class person. The genius of the first belongs to history; that of the second belongs to the future. Artistic activity, which according to Proust is the only one that justifies human existence, is present everywhere in *Remembrance of Things Past* in filigree. No doubt there are a number of people in the novel who live regular lives and have a profession—Saint-Loup is an officer, Bloch's father a financier, M. de Vaugoubert an ambassador etc.—but we only hear about it incidentally and it is always during their spare time that we meet them. If they work, we have the impression that it is "outside," that there is something clandestine about it like the widows of small time employees who suffer extreme want and who go and do "housework" far away from their own district so that their neighbors will know nothing about it. If we except the "creators," whose work is above ordinary work we find that people who work officially in Proust, such as the narrator's father, are the oddest group in the novel like those sympathetic characters who are bowled over by unstinted praise in two or three lines and then disappear for ever from the book.[1] But we should observe that even if they are idle, all the other characters are extraordinarily occupied. Charlus's days are as full of calculations and maneuvers as Napoleon's. Now it is in the midst of this contradictory agitation that the favorite prey for Proustian penetration is seen to flourish. His domain is the comedy that the man performs for himself in order to make himself interesting, even when he is genuinely interesting. Thus Charlus tries to make himself interesting when he is already interesting, but interesting without knowing it, and obviously for other reasons than those he wishes. According to Proust's teaching, lucidity might be defined as knowing oneself to be interesting or uninteresting for reasons which make one genuinely so. Even a man who works for fifteen hours a day may feel the need to mimic to excess his actual activity with the idea of giving his life an importance of its own, presenting it to other people while actually living it, in the form of a story that is being related and consequently stylized. It follows that the fact that someone is very active does not prevent him from behaving as though he were idle. There exists in everyone a form of activity which always drives him, even if he finds himself in the most harrassing circumstances, to divert a proportion of the energy which is essential to the maintenance of his position and his health, in order to devote it to playing a part. Only Proust's characters represent this form of comedy in its pure state because what is important, what is of absolutely capital importance for them, is the exact equivalent of a total vacuum. Saint-Simon also describes idle people, but he does not judge them as such for the simple reason that he believes in the aristocracy. Proust's cruelty is therefore not like Saint-Simon's the result of badness of character or even of moral indignation which for that

[1] *E.g.* the exquisite, perfect, charming Luxembourg-Nassau, a character who is only mentioned once. (II, p. 539, *The Guermantes Way*: I, p. 1100 (RH); VI, p. 316 (C&W).

102, 206

matter is often justified in Saint-Simon. One has no scruples about monumentalising peoples' follies when they really make no sense. The idleness of the characters in *Remembrance of Things Past* is not therefore an accident of social circumstance; it is less still the fact of belonging to a particular class than the basic element which is necessary for the appearance of those aspects of human nature that Proust describes. It is Proust's *subject*. And what is a great writer if he is not the person who discovers a subject?

Having shown that the nobility is no more than a section of the *haute bourgeoisie* which stands out against it simply as a result of its idiosyncrasies and additional obsessions, Proust knows how to take advantage of the element of hypertrophy that idleness brings to these idiosyncrasies. Thus he underlines the opposition between the gentle, reserved attitude of the Prince de Borodino—who belongs to the nobility of the Empire and who in the comparatively recent past performed important state functions—and the derisory ballet danced on its own account by the aristocracy of Ancien Régime who through its heredity had completely lost all idea of what constitutes responsibility. This explains in a decidedly retrospective fashion the naïveté and incompetence of a Chateaubriand, a Polignac, a Chambord, when they were accidentally brought into contact with active political policy. As for passive political policy, the nobility, as we can see from its behavior during the Dreyfus case, simply plays the part of the most reactionary wing of the upper middle class. Proust demolishes once for all the ancient legend: the fundamental mediocrity of the Duchesse de Guermantes and her spitefulness are one of the most crushing conclusions of the book. Only a Charlus escapes mediocrity and that is the effect of his lunacy to which he owes the "*étroite brèche qui donne jour sur Beethoven et sur Véronèse* (narrow loophole that opens upon Beethoven and Veronese)."[1] But Charlus, who is "full of genius" when he talks, if he had been a writer would probably have produced insipid sentimental novels instead of that delicious repertoire of terms of which his superior sense of language would have made him capable together with his prodigious

[1] III, p. 206; *The Captive*: II, p. 524 (RH); X, p. 280 (C&W).

verbal memory—"*Génial* Charlus" whose element of genius is precisely what remains unrecognized by the socialites.

A day to day understanding of other people is the result of Proust's essential preoccupation: truth. If the search for truth seems to end in failure, or at any rate in a sort of exhaustion, it was because Proust was able to reject in this context every brilliant theory that has come to adorn those things of which he was sure, and in this way the truths he had discovered fit in so well with his usual manner of perceiving that for him they no longer have any attraction and merge into the findings of everyday life. One might perhaps by following Proust's example define maturity as the capacity for enjoying an everyday life which is as free from depression as it is from exaltation, or rather in which exaltation and depression are not the only means of avoiding boredom. Notably, Proust is the first and up to the present the only great writer in any literature who is absolutely a-religious. He is not even anti-religious. He does not seek to combat religion by means of a metaphysic which adopts the form of religion while refuting it, and in order to deny it appeals to those very instincts in man which nourish religion. He is from the start free from all prejudice and in no sense to be suspected of harboring some hidden taste for the transcendental or the moral, which saves him from any setback or compensatory aggressiveness. He does not fight any more than he profanes (Voltaire fought, Sade profaned). He knows nothing of this. While Gide's only theme remains the conflict between a super-self still completely impregnated with the idea of traditional morality, and freedom ("I am a little boy who amuses himself and at the same time a Protestant pastor who is bored"), Proust begins at the point where the memory of a conflict has already been relegated to prehistory. In this way he is able to tackle directly what is perhaps in his eyes the most important problem of all: the problem of the true nature and the possible truth of our personal relations with other human beings: "*Comment a-t-on le courage de souhaiter vivre, comment peut-on faire un mouvement pour se préserver de la mort, dans un monde où l'amour n'est provoqué que par le mensonge?* (How have we the courage to wish to live, how can we

move a finger to preserve ourself from death in a world in which
love is provoked only by falsehood?)".[1]

In the society which he paints for us and in which, as
soon at it is a question of moral truths, the majority of peo-
ple prefer knowing less to trying to justify themselves, where
they are tormented without being uneasy, nervous without
really being preoccupied, where they only perceive in the act
of learning the unpleasant fact of not having known, where
each person willingly accuses himself of error rather than
having recourse to the means of no longer having to commit
it, where indifference alone engenders impartiality and in
consequence makes it sterile, where contact with other people
is therefore in every sense of the term extremely "limited"
owing to a general absence of curiosity, the narrator of *Remem-
brance of Things Past* offers us the example of a man capable of
spending long hours thinking exclusively about somebody else—
and often even about somebody else who has no direct relation
with his own immediate preoccupations.

He is continually divided between the desire for an existence
where other people would scarcely count for us and above all
would not be able to disappoint us and cause us suffering, and
the need for an existence whose meaning on the contrary would
depend entirely on another person. He has been attracted in
turn by loyalty to an inner and slightly mythical "fatherland"
(and he takes up again on his own account the naïve Bergsonian
distinction between the "superficial" and the "deeper" self)
and the need to become passionately interested in other beings.
Literary work alone will satisfy both these needs at the same
time, but it will only do so after Proust has tried, in the real
world, to satisfy each of them in turn without managing to do so
completely. People often speak about one of these two aims: the
one moving in an interior direction, towards the *"vrai moi"*
(true self). But they emphasise less often because, as Proust tells
us, it makes him live and vibrate instead of outlining the pro-
gram and solemnly announcing its principle and its benefits,
that before embarking on his work, the main thing from the

[1] III, pp. 94–5; *The Captive*: p. 443 (RH); X, p. 120 (C&W).

beginning to the end of the book to which he looks for salvation
and which guides his life, is love.

IF IT IS ABSOLUTELY CERTAIN that "the important thing is to
love," Proust none the less and for that very reason ends up in a
discouraging pessimism. For in the last resort every attempt to
escape from ourselves and to depend sincerely on another per-
son can only produce suffering. In fact, for Proust really to love
means to suffer: to become conscious of suffering at the moment
when it is too late to draw back:

> *Swann tout d'un coup aperçut en lui l'étrangeté des pensées qu'il roulait*
> *depuis le moment où on lui avait dit chez les Verdurin qu'Odette était déjà*
> *partie, la nouveauté de la douleur au coeur dont il souffrait . . . Il fut bien*
> *obligé de constater que dans cette même voiture qui l'emmenait chez Prévost*
> *il n'était plus le même, et qu'il n'était plus seul, qu'un être nouveau était là*
> *avec lui, adhérent, amalgamé à lui, duquel il ne pourrait peut-être pas se*
> *débarrasser, avec qui il allait être obligé d'user de ménagements.*

> Swann suddenly perceived how foreign to his nature were the
> thoughts which he had been revolving in his mind ever since he
> had heard at the Verdurins' that Odette had left, how novel the
> heartache from which he was suffering, but of which he was only
> now conscious . . . He was obliged to admit also that now, as he
> sat in the same carriage and drove to Prévost's, he was no longer
> the same man, was no longer alone even—but that a new
> personality was there beside him, adhering to him, amalgamated
> with him, a creature from whom he might, perhaps, be unable to
> liberate himself, towards whom he might have to adopt some . . .
> stratagem.[1]

A sentence which is echoed by another at the end of *Cities of
the Plain* when after the night on which he had come to see that
he could never do without Albertine, a weeping Proust watches
the sun rising over the sea through the window of his hotel bed-
room:

> *Je me rappelai l'exaltation que m'avait donnée, quand je l'avais aperçue*
> *duc hemin de fer, le premier jour de mon arrivée à Balbec, cette même image*
> *d'un soir qui ne précédait pas la nuit, mais une nouvelle journée. Mais*
> *nulle journée maintenant ne serait plus pour moi nouvelle, n'éveillerait*

[1] I, p. 228; *Swann's Way*: I, p. 175 (RH); II, p. 14 (C&W).

plus en moi le désir d'un bonheur inconnu, et prolongerait seulement mes souffrances—jusqu'à ce que je n'eusse plus la force de les supporter. I remembered how thrilled I had been when I had seen from the railway on the day of my first arrival at Balbec, the same image of an evening which preceded not the night but a new day. But no day would be new to me any more, would arouse in me the desire for an unknown happiness; it would only prolong my sufferings, until the point when I should no longer have the strength to endure them.[1]

But why this pessimism? It is not that love is harmful or fatal in itself. Proust is in no sense a romantic; he does not work out a metaphysic of love. On the contrary, he remains firmly in the domain of complete empiricism: in itself and by itself love is truly happiness; and if it isn't, it's because "it doesn't work out." Admirable humility! " '*Etre près des gens qu'on aime,' dit M. de Charlus, citant La Bruyère, 'leur parler, ne leur parler point, tout est égal'* ('To be close to the people whom one loves,' said M. de Charlus, quoting La Bruyère, 'to talk or not to talk to them is all the same')." And he added: " '*Il a raison, c'est le seul bonheur, et ce bonheur-là, hélas, la vie est si mal arrangée, qu'on le goûte bien rarement* (He is right; that is the only form of happiness and that happiness—alas, life is so ill arranged that one very rarely tastes it)."[2]

We enjoy it, in fact, only through the chance of a "coincidence," which is illusory and provisional, between the need we have of a person and the need that the person might have of us, of those "coincidences which are so perfect, when reality falls back and applies itself to what we have dreamed about for so long." But in order to be happy, we must never reach the degree of attachment where "the beloved is in turn the malady and the remedy which suspends and aggravates the malady." A formula, however, which is the very formula of happiness, so true is it that "*il est humain de chercher la douleur et aussitôt de s'en délivrer* (it is human to seek pain and at once to cure oneself of it)".

[1] I, p. 228; *Cities of the Plain*: II, pp. 364–5 (RH); pp. 364–5 (C&W).
[2] I, p. 763; *Within a Budding Grove*: I, p. 577 (RH); IV, p. 85 (C&W).

It has often been said that in Proust love is an accident. But on the contrary, he only takes pleasure in exaggerating the accidental nature of the thousand circumstances which surround the birth of a passion in order to bring out more clearly that passion in itself is the strongest accentuation of life.

Thus Proust might have adopted on his own account the sentence that Kierkegaard in *Either/Or* attributes to the supposed author of the *Diapsalmata*:

> Alas! The door of happiness does not open inwards, and therefore it does not help to throw oneself at it in order to force it; it opens outwards and there is nothing one can do about it.

With this difference, that he himself never said "alas."

In the first place, he believes in happiness, in life, in everything that is positive. He does not teach that suffering is a good thing, that defeat is profitable, illusion more precious than reality. He attaches himself to others as much as to himself; to things as much as and more than to his "states of consciousness" in relation to things; to the content of his vision more than to the vision itself, which is the reverse of the narcissistic novelists like Dostoyevsky whose aim before all else is to project "their" own light on to things. Proust's characters are never the result of a hallucinatory projection, but always of a meeting. Their intensity comes from themselves and not from his obsessions about them. Proust is sometimes misinterpreted in the same way as Montaigne. On the pretext that Montaigne sometimes presents himself to the reader as the analyst of his own "ego," they appear not to notice that in the *Essays* he speaks more about what he sees around him than about himself and that even when he says "I," it is in fact a way of arriving at what "I" have seen or read *outside* himself. Unlike so many writers who though talking about what is external to them, in the end never talk about anything but themselves, Montaigne, though speaking about himself, cannot prevent himself from talking about things which are external to him. In this unconquerable emergence from oneself, the writer whom together with Montaigne Proust seems to me to resemble most closely (he is already linked to him by his hatred

of the small-time *bel-esprit* and false mystery) by his visual
acuteness in the instantaneous perception of the comic element
that surrounds him—a perception which always demands
forgetfulness of self—is Molière.

Proust often said that literary work proceeded from a self
which was not the "social" self of everyday life. In asserting this,
he was following the philosophical fashion of his day and he
meant to react against the aesthetic of Sainte-Beuve without
perceiving that it might have been simpler to refute Sainte-
Beuve by pointing out that his error did not consist in trying to
explain literature by life, but first and foremost in a failure to
understand life.

For in the last resort, if one had to choose a book which
proved that the opposition between life and the work, between
art and reality, is of no importance and which demonstrated on
the contrary not so much their identity, to be sure, but their
unity, would it not be, in spite of all his theories, Proust's own
book that we should have to nominate?

II

Sois-moi mondaine
Je suis ton daim.

Be worldly with me;
I am your buck.

MAX JACOB

Chapter II

PROUST AGAINST THE SNOBS

——————

W E ARE SNOBS when our attitude to a human being (I leave aside snobbery towards animals, a complex subject on which, I am told, several doctoral theses are in course of preparation) does not depend directly on a particular person or on the impression that his presence makes on us, but on a third force which is foreign to the qualities and failings which belong to him personally. The third factor may be nobility, money, power, the possession of a car which exceeds a certain speed, a horse, a dog, a sporting or a literary reputation, or even a university title; membership (past, present or future) of some corporate body: school, administration, association, army. Or, again, it may depend on the fact that he stayed in this or that country, town, or even hotel; on having gone in for hunting, shooting, fishing, skiing, Alpine mountaineering, yachting, the white slave traffic, a foreign language; on having been present at congresses or (in other milieux) on having been a thief, a murderer or done time in prison. Man finds grounds for snobbery in everything. Thus, when in the company of drug addicts, one might find oneself witnessing the contempt of opium-smokers for morphiomaniacs, or of morphiomaniacs for ether-drinkers, etc.

In a large town in Texas there is a district where, as a result of a tacit understanding between landowners and real estate agents, nobody ever sells an inch of land to people whose fortune is valued at less than a million dollars. Now, from a strictly practical point of view, the "residential" and luxury aspect of the district could certainly be preserved at a lower price. What conditions it in this instance is an image, a totem, an exclusiveness,

which for that matter is something that happens in so many
American cities where only a few yards separate that part of
the city where it is good form to live from that part where
residence would mean your exclusion from a certain society
notwithstanding the fact that, so far as the eye can see, there is
no difference in the attractiveness or the cleanliness of the two
sectors of the district, which are next door to one another, and
that only the difference in the rents or prices marks the passage
from one to the other.

It would be easy and fastidious to extend the list. The essential
thing is that an idea is interposed between ourselves and our
fellows and hangs over our heads. No matter if the person to
whom we happen to be talking shows the most blatant signs of
stupidity and vulgarity; they do not register with us as such
because we are dominated by the knowledge that he is a fencing
champion, a contributor to *Time* magazine, a French ambassador
or the head of Girard's lollipop business. The most boring per-
son does not bore us any longer. Through him we come into
contact with the Idea and, as M. Verdurin remarks, he is "in"
(note the vocabulary of magical or Platonic participation). At
the very end of the novel, Mme Verdurin, now Princesse de
Guermantes and almost moribund (because for the snob like
the politician there is no retirement age) cries: "Yes, that's it,
we will forgather! We will summon the clan! I love this younger
generation, so intelligent, so ready to join in! Ah! what a
mujishun you are!"[1] Right up to the last, as the author ob-
serves, she was determined to "join in," to "summon the
clan."

Among the crudest grounds of discrimination are first, aris-
tocratic or official titles, power and money. But it would be
possible to draw up a list of millions of other principles of dis-
crimination. The more complicated a civilization grows, the
more diverse the criteria of snobbery become—with wealth and
power going by the board, at any rate in appearance—the more
snobbery multiplies its facets, turns out to be changeable, sub-
divides, disguises itself and goes as far as to turn itself inside out.

[1] *The Past Recaptured*: p. 221 (RH); p. 384 (C&W).

The anti-snobbery of the snobs is nothing in fact except a variety of snobbery which Proust catalogues in the same way as other things when he writes, for example, that the Duchesse de Guermantes *"reprit son point de vue de femme du monde, c'est-à-dire de contemptrice de la mondanité* ([resumed] the normal point of view of a society woman, the point of view, that is to say, of a woman who affects to despise society)."[1]

In other societies snobbery remains robust and simple: it needs distinctive systems of etiquette, visible signs. In Italy, a person is condemned to an inferior existence if he is without a title, if he is reduced to himself. It is always a last resource, a sign of rudeness, simply to address some one as "Sir." He must be Doctor, Engineer, Commander, Barrister, Professor, Accountant, etc. The story is told of an unfortunate man who was run over by a lorry and killed because for fear of vexing him a passer-by who had seen the danger dared not shout a warning by addressing him simply as *"Signore!"* He took a chance and called him *"Commendatore!"* The victim, not being a commander, did not look round and lost his life. Every form of snobbery is based on a preliminary conformity without which it would be swamped and in a perpetual state of confusion. It therefore assumes the uncritical acceptance of certain values. The blindness of the acceptance can go as far as to make us admit a religious respect for a social hierarchy from which we ourselves are in fact excluded. It is the snobbery of servants, so well described by Proust. It is also in the societies of the great landowners the worship of the peasants for their masters and the practices of which they are the victims. The need to be classed, even if it means being placed in the lowest class, makes men cherish any form of class distinction.

Snobbery recomposes, inside a circle limited by an artificial frontier, the entire scale of human qualities and feelings. Outside the circle a person may possess virtues, be kind or intelligent, but to use the language of the bureaucrats, he will never be given the "title" of these virtues. Conversely, "kindness," "courage," "brilliance," etc., grow infinitely if they flourish in

[1] III, p. 1023; *The Past Recaptured*: p. 252 (RH); p. 438 (C&W).

an ambassador who subscribes to the Idea. A boy who is "very brilliant," "very cultivated," "very musical," "very upright," "very funny," etc., does not speak, express himself or conduct himself in the same way, with the same intonation, the same urgency with the holder of a title as he does with someone who is without an official position. The establishment of a title will depend as much on a whole social class as on a group reduced to a handful of people or even a single family. We know the kind of auto-snobbery that unites members of certain families in mutual admiration which is as tough as it is unmotivated and which indeed sometimes fails to prevent them from tearing one another to pieces. It matters little: by dividing humanity into those who are "in" and those who are not, snobbery makes life easier for us; it frees us from the obligation to feel and pass judgement in each particular case, and it joins our self-respect to the boundless respect that we display towards a limited number of other individuals.

EVERY CATEGORY OF SNOBS therefore suggests a secret society whose cohesion depends on the fierce protection of a non-existent treasure. In calling the treasure "non-existent," I am obviously speaking of the justifications and the pretexts that snobbery assumes in the field of moral, intellectual or aesthetic values. At bottom, the treasure does indeed exist because every form of snobbery defends, at any rate in its beginnings, the interests of a class, a group, a clan or a coterie. In the last analysis, in the microscopic scale, there is only one form of snobbery: money and its equivalents—power, influence, fame. But there is a very large gap between what we might call the root of an attitude and its proliferation. As Marx showed in *The 18th Brumaire of Louis Napoleon*, every moral system acquires a sort of autonomous power which is more durable than the causes that inspired it. It can survive the necessities which gave rise to it, or which it resisted, and influence in turn its own supports by developing on its own account and more wildly.

By swamping on a large scale its most classic forms like so-called fashionable life and its monstrous forms like anti-semitism and racialism, snobbery becomes fathomless and polymorphous. It is always present in everybody, whether in the form of an imperceptible residue, and subtly corrupts our attitudes. It falsifies the behavior even of people who set their faces against it most firmly (there is a snobbery inside the Communist Party and, of course, inside the Catholic Church), or who in an attempt to defend themselves gauchely adopt the opposite standpoint in which we can read, in its entirety like the reflection in a mirror of back-to-front handwriting, this admission: fraternising with low company obviously means that you are a snob. Snobbery colors all personal relations in law-abiding societies because it reproduces to the fullest extent permitted by law and interest that vast edifice of inclusions and exclusions in which ethnology has discovered a phenomenon that is fundamental to every form of society. One is snobbish towards a person whom, in certain archaic social systems where there only exist two categories of human beings, relations and enemies, one would normally kill.

As the detector and extremely accurate recorder of the faintest traces of snobbery to be found in nature, whether crystallized, fossilized, liquefied or gaseous, Proust perceives their ubiquity, mimicry and ramifications. He amuses himself without ever growing tired by deciphering, with the help of an anti-snobbery grid invented by himself, their purpose and their actions. Wherever he happens to be, the first thing that his eye and his sensibility perceive in the people he is watching is the dark nook in which the secret behind the grimace is palpitating. He at once fixes on the secret, isolates it, drives it to the wall and enjoys watching the holder or the candidate for the position working himself up, interminably retracing the triangular route which takes him from the person or persons present to the Value of which he is the slave, returning at last, after consulting this Value, to his own feelings (if one can put it like that).

Sometimes Proust even prolongs the experiment and sadistically tortures the snob. He lets Mme de Cambremer, who is an intellectual snob, give herself away by her condemnation of Poussin who she imagines is always out of fashion. Then he remarks, casually, that Degas is very fond of the Poussins at Chantilly:

"Ouais?" répondit-elle. "Je ne connais pas ceux de Chantilly . . . mais je peux parler de ceux du Louvre, qui sont des horreurs." "Il les admire aussi énormément." "Il faudra que je les revoie. Tout cela est un peu ancien dans ma tête," répondit-elle après un instant de silence, et comme si le jugement favorable qu'elle allait certainement bientôt porter sur Poussin devait dépendre, non de la nouvelle que je venais de lui communiquer, mais de l'examen supplémentaire et cette fois définitif, qu'elle comptait faire subir aux Poussin du Louvre, pour avoir la faculté de se déjuger.

"Indeed? I don't know the ones at Chantilly," said Mme de Cambremer, ". . . but I can speak about the ones in the Louvre, which are appalling." "He admires them immensely too." "I must look at them again. My impressions of them are rather distant," she replied after a moment's silence, and as though the favourable opinion which she was certain, before very long, to form of Poussin would depend, not upon the information that I had just communicated to her, but upon the supplementary and, this time, final examination that she intended to make of the Poussins in the Louvre in order to be in a position to change her mind.[1]

And in her dreamy look, we see already the dawn of a sudden change of view which in a fortnight's time will infallibly lead her to admire Poussin. Morel himself, who is so weak and so little affected by the contempt of other people, also has an Achilles heel: the sacrosanct violin class at the Conservatoire. The whole world can take him for a dirty little cad for all he cares—the only thing that worries him is the fear that something might come out about him at the rue Bergère.

What blindness has sometimes prompted people to treat Proust as a society novelist who though exceptional is still a novelist whose chief merit is to have extracted something profound from the superficial, to have transformed ungrateful material into something human—a sort of Saint-Simon of the upper middle class?

Saint-Simon believes in the reality of the aristocracy of the blood, but every day he is struck by their paltriness and their misdeeds which are like a bombshell to his faith in them, rock it

[1] II, p. 813; *Cities of the Plain*: II, p. 153 (RH); VII, p. 297 (C&W).

to its very foundations, make its moral system untenable. This explains the bitterness and ferocity, the sardonic indignation of the *Memoirs*. Where Saint-Simon-Alceste suffers, Proust-Philinte is all irony, sensitive to the sheer oddity of people. Some people claim that Proust describes aristocratic and society life because it is interesting in itself; others think that being half-Jewish he was fascinated by something to which he would never really have been admitted. These two interpretations would be perfectly proper on the part of people who had never opened *Remembrance of Things Past*. If the first of them is correct, it is equally correct to say that *La Farce de Maître Pathelin*[1] is a study of the state of the Law in the fifteenth century. As for the second, it is the result of the unimaginative application of scraps of psychoanalysis which maintain that everything we do is designed to defend us against a strong inclination to do the opposite, or to delude ourselves by concealing our irritation at not being able to do it. Cervantes probably harbored a secret love and a nostalgic tenderness for novels of chivalry. But Proust's tone does not deceive. There is no hint of affection at the heart of his satire. Besides, it is not a matter of simple satire in his case, which would amount to an assumption that the author had begun by taking seriously the things at which he is now tilting. For if it were no more than that, we should not be able to understand why we can always re-read with the same pleasure the same pages about the stupidity of M. de Norpois or the sly selfishness of the Guermantes, nor why readers who have never met specimens of these social types take an interest in Proust's descriptions of them. In order to bite, "demystification" presupposes mystification. The force of Proustian satire like Molière's satire on preciosity is linked to something else and thrusts its roots much more deeply into the ground trodden by the individuals at whose expense it is exercised. *Remembrance of Things Past* is neither a novel intended to compensate the disappointed or persecuted snob nor even the chronicle of the

---

[1] The authorship of this play, which was written in 1464 and is sometimes described as "the first French comedy," is uncertain, but it may have been by a Norman priest-poet named Guillaume Alexis. *Tr.*

twilight of a society: the cruel and skeptical description of social life at which the experienced pen of Mme Gyp excelled— the novelist whom Nietzsche prized so highly—or the spiteful, nagging pen of the Goncourts whose diary sounds in this domain the hour of disillusion, the discarding of the masks and the appearance of the twitches. Proust never had to discover the limits of the "polite world" because he never believed in the "polite world." More precisely, he believed in the wit, in the charm of the "polite world" before he came to know it, and his illusions vanished at the very moment of his first contact with reality. Chapter II of *The Guermantes Way* (if one can speak in the case of Proust of genuine "chapters"), "The wit of the Guermantes, as displayed before the Princesse de Parme," is written expressly for that reason. His letter to Reynaldo Hahn, in which he derides the Parisian Egerias and does a pastiche of the style of their party invitations, shows that the man who at the age of twenty contributed to the *Revue Blanche* did not have to withdraw after a period in "polite society." It is unusual, however, to find readers of Proust who do not believe that *Remembrance of Things Past* contains at the same time as criticism a discreet admission of admiration and a melancholy farewell.

This amounts to confusing Proust with, for example, Gabriel Louis Pringué, the sympathetic author of *Trente ans de dîners en ville*. Pringué believes in the "polite society," in the perfect image that people who never entered it formed for themselves in 1900. Although he did enter it, he looks on it in the same way that they did. For him the salons are peopled by women who are "devilishly" pretty (the adverb is his); the queens always display a queenly bearing; fashionable authors make their entry by "throwing out three or four witty remarks" in exactly the same way that children imagine that the hero of a Western never makes a move without firing a few pistol shots. The duchesses are always very "good," the marchionesses have a gift for repartee which is enough to fell an ox for you. Pringué quotes ecstatically a large number of "witty remarks" and "repartees" which were famous in the fashionable society of five continents between 1900 and 1914, which are so exasperatingly

inept and in which it is impossible to discover even in their
foetal stage the tiniest hint of anything really witty, with the
result that his book runs the risk of being taken one of these days
for a melancholic man's indictment in the manner of Tacitus's
Annals.

On the moral plane, Pringué believes that there are good
people who are wholly good and bad people who are wholly
bad, as there are in the *chansons de geste* and the Westerns. The
fact of the matter is that Pringué has written a sort of Western
about fashionable society. He believes in the virtues of men of
the world as a child is certain in advance that Davy Crockett or
Billy the Kid will always be brave and will never miss their
target. Alas! virtue does not always triumph. We only have to
read the shattering page in which Pringué indulges in a long
lamentation over the fact that newly arrived ladies without any
legitimate position in society manage to work their way, simply
on account of their money, into the presidencies of charitable
societies and organizations for good works.

Lastly, on the metaphysical plane, to belong to what he calls
the "upper crust of society" is, according to Pringué, a guaran-
tee that the person possesses the qualities of intelligence, beauty
and goodness which are inherent in the individuals themselves
and inalienable (in the same way that the Scholastics thought
that Dryness, Humidity, Warmth and Cold were properties
belonging to the very essence of certain bodies). When speaking,
for example, of a woman who is "*diablement jolie*," he writes:
"Her figure was the figure of a genuine statue." Thus for
Pringué (1) there exist genuine and false statues; (2) only
genuine statues have a good figure; (3) women who do not
belong to the "upper crust of society" resemble false statues.

They are, of course, all points of view which must be ascribed
to simplicity rather than to malice. I shall not dwell any longer
on a writer to whom I intend later on to devote a full-length
study.

Although too brief, these *aperçus* do at least enable us to say
that Proust's book is more than the converse of Pringué's.
Remembrance of Things Past does not bear the same resemblance

to *Trente ans de dîners en ville* that *Don Quixote* does to *Amadis*; in the present context, as in many others, it is much more the converse of *La Comédie humaine*. For when it is a question of believing in the fundamental excellence of individuals who comprise the nobility, in the superiority of the human substance of the women of the Faubourg Saint-Germain, Balzac displays a simple faith. As for Saint-Simon, he has to go as far as the Spanish court in order to find an etiquette after his own heart, a ceremonial whose visible ordering reflects and translates into material terms the inequalities of rank and blood, so true is it that the snobbish dream is to realise in external objects and to demonstrate by the choice of uniforms the hierarchy that he would like to believe is founded on human nature itself. Driven on by the obsession that rank depends on the place to which one has a right in the chapel or at a ceremony, on the right to keep one's hat on, to cross or not to cross a threshold—in short, on topography—Saint-Simon goes as far as to write: "Madrid is a great and handsome city whose unequal situation, much of it standing on a very steep slope, has perhaps given rise to the kind of distinction of which I am about to speak."[1] At the opposite pole, Proust does not even attempt to justify society life, as people often do, by setting out to show that, without deserving it, the snobs nevertheless serve as ornaments, useless but delightful, in any well-ordered society. No novel destroys more simply than his the legend that leisure, wealth and confinement within a narrow circle of personal relationships create the conditions which favor the flowering of qualities of mind and elegance of manners. In a sketch for the character of Charlus, in which he is known as M. de Quercy, we read: "He went to Paris. He was in his twenty-fifth year, extremely good-looking and, *for a man of fashion, witty.*"[2] After the lack of wit, ignorance: "*the extraordinary ignorance of all these people*"—the people who in *Time Regained* are present at the Princesse de Guermantes' morning party.[3] Thus it is not simply out of psychological interest, but

[1] *Memoirs*, Ch. LXVI.
[2] *By Way of Sainte-Beuve* (italics mine).
[3] III, p. 1002; *The Past Recaptured*: p. 236 (RH); p. 409 (C&W).

out of an ethnological curiosity that Proust describes in detail and reproduces mercilessly the manner of speech of the people of fashion. The language of people who are false is always false in itself because it has no natural center and, not flowing from any source, is made up of close fitting scraps like the streams of silver paper in Provençal cradles. The bad French of the Duc de Guermantes (Françoise's "bloomers" are preferable) when so many working class people like Jupien, for example, speak perfectly naturally a correct and elegant language, does not, however, fill us with the same *malaise* as the vulgarities of vocabulary and syntax, the mixture of learned words misunderstood, the chunks of slang, the familiar and affected expressions, the suggestive silences, which so many society people seem to use in order to excuse themselves for not possessing either a language or a tongue and which we find in the propositions put to the narrator by Gilberte de Saint-Loup:

> *Mais comment venez-vous dans ces matinées si nombreuses? . . . Vous retrouver dans une grande tuerie comme cela, ce n'est pas ainsi que je vous schématisais? Certes, je m'attendais à vous voir partout ailleurs qu'à un des grands tralalas de ma tante, puisque tante il y a . . .*
> But how do you come to be at a party of this size . . . To find you at a great slaughter of the innocents like this doesn't at all fit in with my picture of you. In fact, I should have expected to find you anywhere rather than at one of my aunt's kettle drums, because of course she is my aunt . . .[1]

Proust is as unimpressed as he could be by aristocracy and wealth; as alien as one can be to the idea even of a social élite. Everywhere he exposes the silliness and the vulgarity of society people and if we pay special attention to the demonstration it is because it goes without saying that even though it is continued, it remains in the margin of the story and never itself determines its course. In *The Captive*, however, he is explicit in his declaration of contempt at the moment when he describes the musical evening which Baron de Charlus organises at Mme Verdurin's in honor of Morel. We remember that at the request of the

[1] III, p. 984; *The Past Recaptured*: p. 221 (RH); p. 385 (C&W).

"Patroness" Charlus's invitations were confined almost exclusively to people belonging to his own world who behave so badly that in order to revenge herself, Mme Verdurin persuades Morel at the end of the evening to drop Charlus:

> *Ce qui perdit M. de Charlus, ce fut la mauvaise éducation, si fréquente dans ce monde, des gens qu'il avait invités. Entendant parler de Mlle Vinteuil, plus d'un disait, "Ah! la fille à la sonate? Montrez-la-moi." Un duc pour montrer qu'il s'y connaissait, déclara, "C'est très difficile à bien jouer."*

What ruined M. de Charlus that evening was the ill-breeding—so common in their class—of the people whom he had invited and who were now beginning to arrive . . . Hearing some mention of Mlle Vinteuil . . . more than one of them said: "Ah! The sonata-man's daughter? Shew me her" . . . A Duke, in order to shew that he knew what he was talking about, declared: "It is a difficult thing to play well."

And Proust concludes with these words:

> *Le monde étant le royaume du néant, il n'y a, entre les mérites des différentes femmes du monde, que des degrés insignifiants, que peuvent seulement majorer les rancunes ou l'imagination d'un M. de Charlus.*

The social world being the realm of nullity, there exist between the merits of women in society only insignificant degrees, which are at best capable of rousing to madness the rancors or the imagination of M. de Charlus.[1]

IT IS ALWAYS COMIC to find that a work is regarded obstinately, sometimes for several centuries like Mantegna's *Parnassus*, as a piece of special pleading in favor of the very ideas it set out to refute and the characters whom it represents as being odious or grotesque. One of these days *Das Kapital* may perhaps come to be described as a hymn which shows with veiled sensibility and a tender irony the charm of the working classes' living conditions in the nineteenth century in the same way that at present the term "Proustian" is applied to anyone who cultivates external signs of refinement, to any ephebe at the Quai d'Orsay who whispers a toneless French, to every bluestocking swooning with complications, to every Herculean agitator who invents a

---

[1] III, pp. 245 and 276; *The Captive*: II, pp. 550, 559, 572 (RH); IX, pp. 331, 349, 375 (C&W).

neurosis and though possessing plenty of blood, makes a point of staying in bed until eleven in the evening in order to be more like Proust who was a dying man when he adopted the practice.

In spite of the qualities that he recognizes in her from time to time, the character on whom Proust definitely comes down hardest is the Duchesse de Guermantes. He displays more harshness when finally trampling her underfoot than he shows when crushing the Duke. For the Duke is all of a piece, sharply circumscribed by his titles, his position in society, his pleasures, his money, his selfishness. He makes no pretence of cultivating a different moral code from the one which suits him. The Duchess, on the other hand, is a double agent. Proust begins by displaying towards her the sort of indulgence from which a woman who is practically devoid of wit benefits when acquiring an official reputation in society as the author of witty remarks. The *mot* itself is only responsible for a tenth part of the laughter of those present; the other nine-tenths are due to the powerful social position of the Guermantes who entertain people in the manner in which a good-natured boss manages, during a dinner, to "fuse" the laughter of his employees. For when we look at them carefully, we find that the famous "*mots* of Oriane" are absolutely idiotic. They seldom go beyond a boring play on words. When quoting them, Proust does deliberately what Pringué had done without realising he was doing: he shows what a low price is sufficient to acquire in a social milieu falsified by snobbery the reputation of being a great wit. He cruelly describes in detail the quackery of the Duchess who repeats her own *mots* to a succession of audiences and gives the impression of preventing herself from doing so by pretending to have forgotten them, allowing her hand to be forced by the Duke, for the pair of them work in partnership. They have a single motive, but a thousand pretexts for their preferences and their actions: the Duchess makes out that she is a bohemian, but she marries as though by chance, and with the help of "the family genius," the richest party in France. She claims to be a connoisseur of literature and art, but is only capable of repeating a mass of clichés. (She knows that Proust is a writer and during the

Princesse de Guermantes' party in *Time Regained* she says to him
solemnly: "Ah! I understand, you have come in order to
observe!")

In Proust's Letters to Reynaldo Hahn[1] we can read his pastiches
of the Comtesse Greffulhe which reveal a young Proust who is as
little of a dupe as the future narrator of *Remembrance of Things
Past*. Because Proust has drawn portraits of society people and
"artistic" men of letters, there has been a tendency to confuse
the author and his subject. We forget that if Proust's style is
dense, complex, heavy-laden—or sometimes, at any rate, be-
cause it often has an airy lightness—it always remains perfectly
simple, is essentially and profoundly natural. From beginning
to end there is not a single example in *Remembrance of Things Past*
of affectation or preciosity, not a single archaism or a single
"elegant" turn of speech.

Finally, in the domain in which knowledge of the world
verges on morality, Oriane professes the cult of friendship, but
behaves revoltingly to the dying Swann. Then, after his death,
she is false to his memory when in *The Sweet Cheat Gone* she invites
Gilberte Swann, who by adoption has become Gilberte de
Forcheville, to lunch and insinuates by her attitude that she had
only known the Jew, Charles Swann, very slightly—she who for
years had been his "greatest friend." For the narrator of
Remembrance of Things Past, the Duchesse de Guermantes' charm
existed at a time when he did not yet know her personally, when
she was the beloved creation of his imagination whom he
followed in the street before he had ever spoken to her. But is
it not one of the most deliberate effects of the story that the
charm vanishes at the first dinner, at the very first conversation
with her? All that is left is a nasty snob who believes that she is
everything that she is not, who claims to take an interest in
everything except the one thing which really interests her: her
position in society. For that is the true nature of snobbery; the
snob reduces all values to a single one, at the same time per-
suading himself that he judges every case disinterestedly in the
name of the love of truth and quality with a high idea of human

[1] *Lettres à Reynaldo Hahn* (1956), Nos. LII, LIII, LV and LVI.

nature. Legrandin takes himself for a poet, a lover of nature, a hermit, when in fact he only dreams of being "seen with" this or that person. The Verdurins claim to have set up their salon in accordance with the principle of impartiality, seeking people of true talent, but the artists who stop visiting or, worse still, who die (two unpardonable ways of "leaving") cease at once in their eyes to have any talent at all and become "bores." The Verdurins clearly belong to the supreme category, to auto-snobbery; they are snobs in themselves.

Although snobbery appears to be intransigent and to pay no attention to perennial values, it is in fact a slave to the fluctuations of fortune, situations, celebrity, and is condemned to inflict continual denials on itself. The principal heroes of Proust find themselves at the feet of (or even marry) people to whom twenty years earlier they would not have wished to be introduced. Bloch, Rachel, Gilberte, Odette, Mme Verdurin take the Faubourg Saint-Germain by storm by means of *coucheries* and money. Morel, the most cunning and the most dishonest character in the book, is called as a witness in a law-suit where his high reputation for honorable behavior, acquired through his social contacts, confers on his evidence and his world, in the absence of any proof, an authority which decides the jury's verdict. Why, then, if it is to end like that, so many years of sly cruelties and suffering, so many snobbish lives devoted to the jealous preservation of imaginary principles, so much subtlety and so many tricks used in the pursuit of a shadow whose only existence is that of vain efforts expended as a complete waste in order to grasp it? In Proust's novel snobbery plays the part of a bait. It inveigles men by means of their ambitions, desires and passions into launching themselves into the void, showing in this way the absence of any sense of proportion on their part and any support in the derisory object to which their impulses are directed. This object is nothing less than the hare of which Pascal speaks in the fragment on "Diversions": that hare which one exhausts oneself in chasing all day and which one "would not have bothered to buy."

III

La gaze la tourmentait. Elle en rêvait une qui viendrait de l'Inde, qui ferait autour de son corps des lignes de neige, qui se draperait sur ses mouvements en des plis tristes et longs comme l'abandon du saule vers la terre, avec toute la lourdeur de l'affaissement des choses légères.

Gauze was torture to her. She dreamed of one which would come from India, which would be like lines of snow round her body, which would drape her movements in long, sad folds in the way in which the willow droops towards the ground with all the heaviness of the sagging of light things.

COMTESSE GREFFULHE

Cet Allemand etait fou d'art, de foulards et de poulardes.

That German was mad on art, scarves, and fowl.

MAX JACOB

On pardonne les crimes individuels, mais non la participation à un crime collectif.

We pardon the crimes of individuals, but not their participation in a collective crime.

PROUST, *The Guermantes Way*

Chapter III

PROUST AND POLITICS

I T IS CLEAR therefore from *Remembrance of Things Past* that
instead of refining taste, leisure and money compel a large
number of unfortunate people to occupy themselves against
their will with art—people who if it were not for the need to
save their faces would never have been condemned to such tor-
ture, and at the same time would have spared other people the
necessity of having to listen to them talking about it. Their
penury would have made productions specially designed for
them entirely useless: spineless literature, pre-digested painting,
and in general a sort of retrospective *avant-garde*.

Proust destroys the paradox of the social function of snobs,
the myth of the hereditary purification of taste. He shows that an
aristocratic and upper middle class education leads not to the
Louvre, but to the Galerie Charpentier.[1] A demonstration
which probes all the more deeply because Proust did not assume
at the outset that he was already on the winning side. By
choosing the Duchesse de Guermantes as a sample of the
nobility and the Verdurins as samples of the *grande bourgeoisie*, he
draws a picture of the anti-snobbish snobs free from all pro-
vincialism—the people whom Jacques Émile Blanche calls *le
gratin revolté* (the upper crust of society in revolt).[2] The "patron"
is "nature". The Duchesse de Guermantes says feelingly:
" '*Vous n'aimez pas le monde? Vous avez bien raison, c'est assommant.
Si je n'étais pas obligée!*' ('You don't care for parties? You're very

---

[1] This gallery, which disappeared in 1965, was famous for the social
gatherings at its private views and the lack of rigor of its exhibitions.

[2] *De Gauguin à la Revue Nègre*, 1928, p. 128.

wise, they are too boring for words. If only I hadn't got to go')."[1]
On top of this, Proust satirizes people who have Vinteuil per-
formed at their afternoon parties, who launched Elstir (the
Verdurins chiefly because the nobility confined themselves to
following their example) and who later on will appear to his-
torians (as he often repeats) to have been in advance of their
time, to have protected the arts and behaved like enlightened
Maecenases. All that is true enough and is what gives its value
to a verdict which would be much less important if Proust had
limited himself to portraying the *decadence* of a milieu. Far from
being attributable to the decrepitude of the salons or what
replaces them, *Remembrance of Things Past* destroys the persistent
legend which always drives people to invoke a brilliant social
past, a time when society was really cultured, a golden age of
snobbery. It has a retrospective effect because inversely it is the
imaginary golden age and even the eighteenth century which
are diminished by the present, by the transfiguration and
embellishment of the recent past taking place in front of our
eyes:

> *Nous aimerions avoir connu Mme de Pompadour qui protégea si bien les
> arts, et nous nous serions autant ennuyés auprès d'elle qu'auprès des
> modernes Egéries, chez qui nous ne pouvons nous décider à retourner tant
> elles sont médiocres.*
>
> We should like to have known Mme de Pompadour, who was so
> valuable a patron of the arts, and we should have been as much
> bored in her company as among the modern Egerias, at whose
> houses we cannot bring ourselves to pay a second call, so un-
> interesting do we find them.[2]

Think of Musil. Although his record and his goal are different,
if we take *The Man without Qualities* in its satiric vein, what
excessive simplicity we find in the caricature of a Diotima—that
Viennese Mme Verdurin whose absurdity lies entirely in the
contrast between what she is and the Ideal that she wants to
serve: a Mme Verdurin who is never right, whose tastes, whose
ideas are all absurd; Diotima who nevertheless achieves a comic

[1] II, p. 380; *The Guermantes Way*: I, p. 990 (RH); VI, p. 99 (C&W).
[2] III, p. 569; *The Guermantes Way*: I, pp. 1121–2 (RH); IV, p. 357
(C&W).

existence thanks to the allusive subtlety of Musil's style: a style which is at once diffuse and lapidary, in which profusion and concision are mysteriously blended. It is never by means of style that Proust makes his characters comic, or rather he does not *make* them comic or odious. He could easily have produced nothing but characters like Mme de Cambremer: a poor frightened animal who, one supposes, was bound to prefer *L'Education sentimentale* to *Madame Bovary*, who would have reviled the Italian opera in 1945 and worshipped it without discrimination in 1960; the woman who feels like vomiting at the thought of Chopin when only Bach is in fashion, but goes into a cold sweat when she hears that Chose or Machin has praised "the incomparable piano compositions of Chopin." Or again, he could have produced an overwhelming series of Odette de Crécys listening to Vivaldi with Malraux's *Voix du silence* and all the Skira albums at her elbow. If he had, he would only have impressed the toadies who are quick to stutter and beat a retreat at the least frown on the part of an interlocutor. But by going for the head, by unveiling the impulses which are responsible for the movements of the ringleaders, the cunning people who often fall under other peoples' paws, Proust gets to the bottom of the retrospective—the purely retrospective—prestige of certain of the milieux of the ruling classes; that is to say, they are the parasites of writers and painters and not the other way round. The Maecenases are pimps rather than protectors.

Nor do I understand why people always speak, in art history, of "the action of a Maecenas" when referring to the purchase of something which has been produced by work, whether it is a picture, a piece of furniture, a series of frescoes, or a statue. Unless it can be proved that the artist was on the verge of starvation and that the purchaser was not in the least attracted by the work he ordered and hastened to destroy it, which is rarely the case, to evoke generosity in connection with a commercial transaction because the object happens to be a work of art betrays a profound contempt for art. When I buy a tin of sardines at the grocer's or an oil stove at the ironmonger's, they would both be very cross if I said that I considered myself their Maecenas. Why

is it always with the feeling of being a protector performing an
act of charity that one buys a gouache from a little-known painter
in the firm hope that, as everyone naturally has an unshakeable
confidence in his own taste, its value will go up? The argument
based on uselessness is worthless because an oil stove sometimes
goes wrong and because a perfume or a rosary are equally use-
less. Yet the customers pay very high prices for them with a
feeling of grateful inferiority and respectful guilt. The only
Proustian characters who have a genuine need of art and litera-
ture, the only ones who have acquired a certain competence in
such matters—Swann and Charlus —are people on the side, off
the beaten track, and if they are well looked on in their own
circle it is not on account of their real merit, but for quite differ-
ent reasons. Their influence in the field of art only counts as a
tiny supplementary contribution to their social influence and is
only perceptible provided that it is strong. With snobbery, as
with love, nothing remains once the positive benefits have lost
the charm that both are supposed to transmit to people who
indulge in them. Although he is too hard on Viollet-le-Duc,
Swann is doubly right in saying, when he hears that Odette is
going to visit the château of Pierrefonds with the Verdurins:

> *"Penser qu'elle pourrait visiter de vrais monuments avec moi qui ai étudié*
> *l'architecture pendant dix ans et qui suis tout le temps supplié de mener à*
> *Beauvais ou à Saint-Loup-de-Naud des gens de la plus haute valeur et ne*
> *le ferais que pour elle, et qu'à la place elle va avec les dernières des brutes*
> *s'extasier successivement devant les déjections de Louis-Philippe et devant*
> *celles de Viollet-le-Duc!"*
>
> "To think that she could visit really historic buildings with me,
> who have spent ten years in the study of architecture, who am
> constantly bombarded, by people who really count, to take them
> over Beauvais or Saint-Loup-de-Naud, and refuse to take anyone
> but her; and instead of that she trundles off with the lowest, the
> most brutally degraded of creatures, to go into ecstasies over the
> petrified excretions of Louis-Philippe and Viollet-le-Duc!"[1]

In order to understand that the salons and their goddesses have
always been Verdurinesque, it is sufficient to read the account,
in the fifteenth book of the *Confessions*, of Mme du Deffand who

[1] I, p. 292; *Swann's Way*: I, p. 224 (RH); II, p. 104 (C&W).

filled Rousseau with an overwhelming desire to flee "owing to
the importance that she attached, for good or ill, to the lowest
class of ass-lickers who put in an appearance" and "her craze
for or against everything, which did not allow her to talk about
anything without convulsions." But Proust showed in addition
not only that the assistance given to art and literature by the
leisure classes is an illusion founded on a previous exclusion
(since to take credit for inviting an author to lunch or putting
him up in a shooting lodge or a servant's bedroom assumes that
a society is normal in which writers are by right without a fire
or anywhere to live), but above all he showed that the leisure
class is itself without talent, that in spite of frequent attempts to
justify it, its way of life is not an art. Leaving aside all intel-
lectual criteria, it is the myth of the social hierarchy based on
manners and feelings which is reduced to mincemeat in
Remembrance of Things Past. The politeness of snobs, a sort of
codified ballet, a "professional slant," inside the group, is less a
form of politeness than the right to be coarse when one chooses
with people from outside. The courtesy eventually shown them
must be seen in relation to a previous exclusion, which is a
matter of principle and to which it is understood, without put-
ting it into words, members of the group reserve the right to
return at any time they choose. Although it is the stage of his
evolution when he appears to us in the most favorable light,
the period when he is a "socialist" and a Dreyfusard out of love
with Rachel, Saint-Loup praises his female cousin, Poictiers,
in these terms: " *'C'est une personne qui fait beaucoup pour ses
anciennes institutrices, elle a défendu qu'on les fasse monter par l'escalier
de service'* ('And then she's the sort of woman who does a tre-
mendous lot for her old governesses; she's given orders that
they're never to be sent in by the servants' stair')."[1]

In spite of the Almanac de Gotha, this attitude demonstrates
once again the identity between the ways of reacting and feeling
of the nobility and the *grande bourgeoisie.* For when she learns
that Morel's father had been a manager at the home of the
narrator's grandparents, Mme Verdurin also says: " *'Je suis*

[1] II, p. 147; *The Guermantes Way*: I, pp. 819–20 (RH); V. p. 196 (C&W).

très contente que le père de notre *Morel ait été si bien. J'avais compris qu'il était professeur de lycée*' ('I am delighted to hear that *our* Morel's father holds such a good position. I was under the impression that he had been a schoolmaster').''[1]

Even if the rules governing inclusion and exclusion are the result of a principle which is totally incomprehensible and indifferent to the person who benefits from one or is subject to the other, the snob's paranoia prevents him from believing in the indifference of the beneficiary or the victim. Hence the scene during which the Duc de Guermantes squeezes the hand of the narrator's father. For actions like streams of feeling really experienced or explicit judgements made about other people, this politeness therefore substitutes the kind of gesticulation of which I have spoken and which surrounds an imaginary treasure hidden in a field, a capering on the point of the toes, executed with the concentration of children "playing at being Indians." Complex and artificial rules are imposed, codified in accordance with a criterion worked out down to the last detail. The criterion is alien to any form of humanity which means that the refinements of the leisure class exclude all delicacy. This explains the worst of the unconscious coarseness when questions and situations arise which are something more than a matter of pure form. I am not thinking here of the inspired insolence of a Charlus which unfortunately has found too many tarted-up imitators who (it was the case, it seems, of a friend of Proust's, Antoine Bibesco) simply indulge in a heavy, vulgar aggressiveness—for one is not mad by choice. Now, the snob may become sympathetic or even genuinely good only when he is mad. It is this that saves Charlus and, on a lower level, Legrandin, that unfortunate errand-boy of the "upper crust of society," always out of breath, whose kind heart gives the narrator the chance of writing that "*le snobisme est une maladie grave de l'âme, mais localisée et qui ne la gâte pas tout entière* (snobbishness is a serious malady of the spirit, but one that is localised and does not taint it as a whole)."[2] Apart from these special cases, which are saved

---

[1] II, p. 910; *Cities of the Plain*: II, p. 221 (RH); VIII, p. 78 (C&W).
[2] III, p. 14; *The Captive*: II, p. 387 (RH); IX, p. 8 (C&W).

by an accidental goodness and a sort of naïve disinterestedness, or again with Charlus by an exceptional verve and even a verbal inventiveness, what is characteristic of the leisure class in the end, as we can see from the use it makes of its leisure, is lack of talent.

In particular, Proust was the first to shed a crude light on the ambiguity of what is known "in polite society" as a brilliant conversation, which hovering between two pictures constantly touches on general, metaphysical, aesthetic and political themes, but is wordy about them without giving any precise information and without any exactness of expression. What allows them to oppose an eventual call to order is the fact that one is not there to tire oneself, that one speaks at "breakneck speed," without pedantry, but without renouncing on that account the advantage of appearing to be taken up with important problems and "knowing about everything." The pseudo *honnête homme* is as incapable of talking in a relaxed manner about rain and fine weather as he is of speaking in a taut fashion about complex questions. This inability to be natural in both cases, in the name of naturalness, leads to a sort of verbal dithering in order to talk uninterestingly about interesting things and in an interesting tone about uninteresting things, to engage in a conversation resembling the manners of a woman of whom somebody—I no longer remember whom—said: "As a marquise she looks more like a *concierge*, but as a *concierge* she looks more like a marquise"; a conversation from which one emerges without being entertained and without having learnt anything, losing on both counts, which arouses in every intelligent man that horrible mixture of profound boredom and mental exhaustion of which Proust himself so often complains. For out of politeness and through being carried along, he does his utmost to shine, but he shines against his own inclination, without serious thought and without really letting himself go, inhabiting and reinforcing in this way a series of "selves" which become lighter and lighter, more and more sterile. In the last resort, what can we hope to learn from a class which is leisured by heredity? What it teaches us without knowing it. And it would be deeply wounded to learn that it is that alone which makes it worthy of attention, while it is in no way so whenever it thinks itself attractive or impressive:

> *Les grands seigneurs sont presque les seules gens de qui on apprenne autant que des paysans; leur conversation s'orne de tout ce qui concerne la terre, les demeures telles qu'elles étaient habitées autrefois, les anciens usages, tout ce que le monde de l'argent ignore profondément.*

> Great noblemen are almost the only people from whom one learns as much as one does from peasants; their conversation is adorned with everything that concerns the land, houses, as people used to live in them long ago, old customs, everything of which the world of money is profoundly ignorant.[1]

It would be more accurate to say: "the class which has recently become monied" into which the great landowners thrust their roots too. For nobody is rich without knowing how to become one of the new rich. The Princesse de Parme possesses a fortune consisting of up-to-the-minute investments. She seems to be saying to herself and her kindly gestures seem to repeat: "Your ancestors were Princes of Clèves and Juliers from the year 647; God has decreed in His bounty that you should hold practically all the shares in the Suez Canal and three times as many Royal Dutch as Edmond de Rothschild . . ." Conversely, the new rich may retain a receptivity, a diversity of individual personalities, a moral sensibility which are lacking in a nobility which for too long has been evened up and hardened by its certainties and its habits:

> *Pour les Juifs en particulier, il en était peu dont les parents n'eussent une générosité de coeur, une largeur d'esprit, une sincérité, à côté desquelles la mère de Saint-Loup et le duc de Guermantes ne fissent piètre figure morale par leur sécheresse, leur religiosité superficielle, qui ne flétrissait que les scandales, et leur apologie d'un christianisme aboutissant infailliblement (par les voies imprévues de l'intelligence uniquement prisée) à un colossal mariage d'argent.*

> Among the Jews especially there were few whose parents and kinsfolk had not a warmth of heart, a breadth of mind in comparison with which Saint-Loup's mother and the Duc de Guermantes cut the poorest of figures by their sereness, their skin-deep religiosity

[1] II, p. 550; *The Guermantes Way*: I, p. 1108 (RH); VI, pp. 331-2 (C&W).

which denounced only the most open scandals, their apology for a Christianity which led invariably (by the unexpected channel of a purely calculating mind) to an enormously wealthy marriage.[1]

This confirms the main idea: finesse is not hereditary, even socially; on the contrary, it becomes degraded with the passing of time, although moral conceptions become steadily narrower and more selfish. It is not among the new rich, but the nobility that it is considered infamous to marry "a convict or (what is worse still) a co-respondent."

IN ORDER TO UNDERSTAND the speed with which the differences between the new rich and the old families are reduced—differences which are to the advantage of the former like those which are to the advantage of the latter—it is sufficient to compare *Remembrance of Things Past* with Thorstein Veblen's classic study, *The Theory of the Leisure Class* (1899). For it is notorious that under cover of a general theory the book contains a specific criticism of American high society in the second half of the nineteenth century: the Vanderbilts, the Goulds, the Harrimans—a class which belonged at that time to the new rich and which was well localized in time and space. It is interesting to observe the precision with which Veblen's analysis follows step by step the description that ten years later Proust will start to give of a leisure class which is infinitely older, situated in a country where the new rich themselves do not have to invent, but find fully worked out and handed down by tradition, the recipes for life that they need. It is unlikely that Proust had ever read or even heard of Veblen (who even today is still virtually unknown in France) and he therefore seems, without abandoning his own original literary method of expression, to owe his perspicacity to a penetration which happened to coincide with certain theories which were contemporary with his work—Veblen's sociology and Freud's psychology—much more than to the systematic and purely rhetorical utilization that he made of philosophies of which he had a more or less direct knowledge—mainly Bergson's.

[1] II, p. 408; *The Guermantes Way*: I, p. 1010 (RH); VI, p. 138 (C&W).

Like Proust's, Veblen's leisure class whose habits consist of what he calls "higher barbarian culture", does not include only individuals who are really inactive. The term "leisure" does not imply immobility or inertia, but the unproductive consumption of time. Also belonging to this class is everybody who devotes himself to activities which have as a common factor the management of men to the exclusion of any form of activity concerned with things, which is a sign of belonging to the middle or lower classes. The man to man activity must of course include an element of authority because mere execution is not sufficient, and we should not be able to include in the leisure class of the "higher barbarian culture" the workers constituting what today are known as the "rank and file." Leisure activities therefore amount generally speaking to the following: political management and high administration, war (or the army in time of peace), the religious profession and sport or hunting, or at any rate the more expensive kinds of sport which demand complicated apparatus and conditions that are only available to a very small number of people because the expenditure of physical energy is admitted solely on condition that it is openly associated with leisure and the spending of money. In certain forms of the development of the "higher barbarian culture" disinterested erudition will have its place among the occupations of the nobility. Of course, even when the activities are lucrative, the lucre must never appear to be the goal in view, and it ought to be patent and plain that the reason for engaging in such activities has nothing whatever to do with earning a living. We need only read with what disgust Saint-Simon speaks of those people who take up a career in order to have "bread" to eat. In Proust, M. de Norpois is the incarnation of the ideal of the man of leisure with a job: ambassador and possessor of a colossal private fortune. As for Swann, he offers the belated combination of money + disinterested erudition (erudition which is paid for reduces the savant to the level of the ridiculous phrasemonger like Brichot who is barely tolerated). As for the person of leisure without a definite occupation—it applies particularly to women—it is a long way from being synonymous with complete repose. We cannot avoid recalling the phrase of Oriane's quoted above ("You don't care for parties? You're very wise, they are too boring for words. If only I hadn't got to go . . .") when we come across the pages in which Veblen analyzes the attitude of "those persons whose time and energy are employed in these matters" (clubs, social life, charitable organizations, etc.) and who "privately avow that all these observances, as well as the incidental attention to dress and other conspicuous consumption, are very irksome but altogether unavoidable."

It is not the only point on which Veblen and Proust are so closely in agreement that we sometimes find them expressing not simply the same ideas, but using the same images and words. For example, Veblen, too, puts down to the credit of the leisure class the fact that it preserves the traditions, the uses and the habits of thought which belong to an archaic cultural scheme. He goes further than Proust when it comes to superior forms of politeness by revealing the deeper reasons for the little ballets danced by the Duc de Guermantes and M. de Charlus, or the secret of the forced benevolence which sugars the face of the Princesse de Parme, manners which are, he says, "a symbolical pantomime of domination on one side and subordination on the other."

The study of the servants of the world of "higher barbarian culture" is equally comic and equally penetrating in both writers—for Veblen is a writer of immense talent—and there are times when we are not sure which of the two we are reading, the sociologist or the novelist. It happens, for example, when the novelist explains why the domestic staff of the leisure class participates itself in the life of the class and by a sort of bias regards itself as a fragment of it because it must of its nature possess characteristics which would make it unsuitable for any other form of employment. Owing to their high degree of specialization and therefore of diversity, the servants are forced to provide continual proof that they are formed exclusively for the work in which they are engaged. The advice given by Saint-Loup to one of his aunt's valets about the tricks he should use to have another valet dismissed all tends towards the organization

of a plot designed to give the victim the appearance of a "lout."
And Veblen:

> It is a serious grievance if a gentleman's butler performs his duties
> about his master's table or carriage in such unformed style as to
> suggest that his habitual occupation may be plowing or shep-
> herding!

Aimé's supereminent dignity, the pride of the Princesse de
Guermantes' "barker," the megalomaniac delirium of the
manager of the Grand Hotel at Balbec on the special day when
he himself cut up the young turkeys, illustrates Veblen's pages
on the servants' participation in the superior standing of the
leisure class. And who can fail to think without emotion of the
mass of Fortuny dresses offered by the narrator to "the Captive"
when he comes across this passage in the chapter in *The Theory
of the Leisure Class* called "Dress as an Expression of the Pecu-
niary Culture":

> . . . the high heels, the skirt, the impracticable bonnet, the corset,
> and the general disregard of the wearer's comfort . . . are so many
> items of evidence that the woman is still, in theory, the economic
> dependent of the man—that, perhaps in a highly idealized sense,
> she is still the man's chattel . . . that [women] are servants to
> whom . . . has been delegated the office of putting in evidence
> the master's ability to pay.

The power of money is for Veblen, too, the only element which
is common to all forms of snobbery. Although it is not always
sufficient in itself to provide immediate access to the leisure
class, it always finishes by taking one there and is the only thing
which enables one to remain. Access may follow a generation
after the acquisition of the money and expulsion may come a
generation after its loss, but no more than that.

THUS PROUST PASSES from social satire to social criticism
simply by emphasizing sharply the features of a description
which is fair both in its delicacy and its element of caricature.
Now that is something which both the novelist and the memoir-

writer must undertake. They are not geologists; they are land-
scape painters, but gazing across their stretch of country we
come to discern the geology of a country. A novelist and a
memoir-writer are no more expected to understand the econo-
mic basis of a society than they are expected in psychology to
know in advance the Freudian complexes; they can discover
both by starting from some detail of everyday life. But they must
then make a spontaneous discovery of them by working out
their own design and not by pretending to work it out while
following a dotted line drawn for them in advance; or when
they only have to apply themselves to sociology, political
economy and medicine. The decision to use peripheral details
as a starting point means that you run the risk of finding some-
thing different from what you expected, if you were expecting
something. If today there no longer exists a revolutionary liter-
ature, it is because writers who are described as left-wing are
under the illusion that it is sufficient to criticize the "infra-
structures," and to respect all the down-at-heel moral and
aesthetic virtues of the middle class. Now, the infrastructures are
a long way down in the earth and do not worry anybody. It is
not them which one perceives. Certain revolutionaries in the
1960s did not like the bourgeois principle, but adored the results.
They willingly frowned on what they took in Proust for indul-
gence towards the disturbing and fetid smells of decadence, but
they found all the Norpoises whom they met "grubbily impres-
sive" and the Mmes de Cambremers delicate, complex, and
highly cultivated—one of those women whom, let us call
things by their names, only the *grande bourgeoisie* can produce. It
seems that today the people who describe themselves as belong-
ing to the left are subject to the criticism that from 1850 to 1930
the bourgeoisie used against itself. It was the work of the most
clear-sighted of its members and made from a point of view
which was essentially moral and psychological, but which led
forcibly to political and social condemnation. No doubt we
should see in this lukewarmness, in this veneration for moral
and religious, literary and stylistic taboos that about 1900 one
hoped would never enjoy any prestige, at any rate in the eyes of

intellectuals, and in the furious speed with which the number of Legrandins multiplied, one of the effects of a long term operation which began in 1930 and which consisted in demanding the revolutionary phraseology while at the same time injecting into it a moral content, an element of fideism and aesthetic naïveté. That is why at present people are content to attack infrastructures: you can say whatever you like about alienation, but nothing about the alienated.

That, too, is why the world satirized by Proust is far from being superannuated. Today, to be sure, there are hardly any salons: they have been replaced by country houses and the "afternoon parties", the *matinées*, have given place to weekends. But underneath the pullover with a polo collar, as in the past underneath the tailcoat, it is the same "revealing heart" that beats. Under the Tourainean or the Norman roof the same conversation goes on, the same clichés disguised as paradoxes; the same affectation of naturalness and innocence hides the equally mechanical gestures and intonations. There is the same implied certainty of representing the same unified standard of the art of living. This is the center of things. The value of the rest of humanity falls when it moves away from this center—a value which is measured by its more or less faithful resemblance to the little gathering which this evening looks at the wood fire and is so discreetly proud of being so much itself. Finally, it is the same fussy, the same overpowering attention in matters of detail, superimposed on a basic incivility, the practice of swamping people with small kindnesses, silly little presents, superfluous telephone calls which go hand in hand with coldness and selfishness.

LIKE TOLSTOY in *Anna Karenina* however, Proust could quite well satirize the leisure class and high officials without deducing from the satire all its historical and political conclusions. The relationship between Proust and Tolstoy is strong, in fact, in their sardonic picture of people of fashion.[1] Tolstoy like Proust

---

[1] Chapters 4 to 7 of Part II of *Anna Karenina* seem to me to be particularly Proustian.

shows simultaneously what the person he is presenting thinks he is and what he really is; the impression that he wants to give of himself as well as the link between his propositions and not what he wants to say, but what he actually does say in spite of himself. The domestic servants are included in Tolstoy in the same way as in Proust. The estate manager Levin is an example.[1] The great difference obviously lies in the fact that Tolstoy is dramatic, tells a story, while in Proust nothing happens. Moreover, apart from his social eye, Tolstoy possesses a direct feeling for natural things, a power of sensation (the admirable day with the harvesters, III, 5 and 6) compared with which Proust's laborious descriptions grow pale. In Tolstoy there is not only something of Proust, but something of Rousseau and unfortunately also something of the fakir. The author of *Anna Karenina* draws spiritual conclusions from his social observations while Proust attaches his to their real roots and extends them by a political *aperçu*.

Politics is present everywhere in *Remembrance of Things Past*, first of all in the Dreyfus case, the moral test of the *belle époque* which hardly ever fails to turn up in any conversation in a salon, a restaurant, on a beach, in an office, an officers' mess, a brothel or a private room; then, later on, in the form of the 1914–18 war in relation to the collapse into a second childhood of the collective intelligence (a phenomenon common to all wars) that it provokes. *Remembrance of Things Past* records the mediocrity of administrative staff by erecting a statue to the pompous stupidity of a Norpois ("all the *althoughs* are misunderstood *becauses*") or the shady careerism of a Bontemps. It sums up the incompetence of the politicians and the General Staff. The recent publication of Abel Ferry's *Carnets secrets* has confirmed the cruel reality of this incompetence at the time when Proust wrote and has demonstrated with what stupidity, with what contempt for human life, the 1914–18 war was conducted. Another classic example of the moral degradation provoked by wars is the move to the right and the war-mongering of the politicians who belonged originally to the left and whose past is

[1] Notably in *Anna Karenina*, Part II, Chapter 13.

forgiven by the right by way of exchange. It is this that sums up the character of Bontemps:

> *Qui eût pu tenir rigueur à Mme Bontemps que son mari eût joué un rôle âprement critiqué par* L'Echo de Paris *dans l'affaire Dreyfus? Toute la Chambre étant à un certain moment devenue révisionniste, c'était forcément parmi d'anciens révisionnistes, comme parmi d'anciens socialistes, qu'on avait été obligé de recruter le parti de l'ordre social, de la tolérance religieuse, de la préparation militaire . . . Bientôt ce nom (de dreyfusard) avait été oublié et remplacé par celui d'adversaire de la loi de trois ans. M. Bontemps était au contraire un des auteurs de cette loi, c'était donc un patriote.*

> Who now could look down on Mme Bontemps because in the Dreyfus affair her husband had played a role which the *Echo de Paris* had sharply criticized? The whole Chamber having at a certain moment become revisionist, it was inevitably from among former revisionists—and also from among former socialists—that the party of social order, of religious tolerance, of military preparedness had been obliged to enlist its recruits . . . But presently this name (of Dreyfusard) had been forgotten and been replaced by that of "opponent of the law of three years' military service." M. Bontemps, far from being its opponent, was one of the sponsors of this law; consequently he was a patriot.[1]

Does it not sound as though we are listening to some one going over the personnel of the Socialist *S.F.I.O.* in 1956? Replace the "Dreyfus case" by "Resistance," Bontemps by Guy Mollet, the law of three years' military service by war in Algeria and the schema remains "valid" (as the *S.F.I.O.* would say). *Time Regained* is a non-acceptance, discreet but firm and unyielding, which is opposed to eye-wash and to chauvinistic emulation.

At a time when all French writers allowed themselves to be more or less enrolled, when Gide's reason tottered, when Valery Larbaud deplored, from his retreat at Alicante, his inability to "serve"; when the unhappy Apollinaire verified the law that in every French poet there is a Déroulède who dozes (and how right Benjamin Péret was, in 1945 in *Le Déshonneur des poètes*, to thrash the resurgence of this phenomenon in the course of the Second World War), it is satisfying to find that the greatest living writer of this period of bloodthirsty incompetence kept

[1] III, p. 976; *The Past Recaptured*: p. 25 (RH); pp. 40-1 (C&W).

his head and never soiled either his conscience or his work with impure themes. It is probably necessary to go as far back into the past as Montaigne in order to find an author who though indifferent to politics when he began writing was forced to occupy himself with it owing to the enormity of the abuses that he witnessed and, in one of those moments in which civilization by a single blow flings to the ground the barriers against barbarism and stupidity, adopts a right attitude by simple moral intransigence and by psychological perspicacity.

The incvitable hypocrisy concealed by a civilized country which performs barbarous acts and is therefore obliged to lie, and to lie to itself, because it is bound to pretend that what it is doing is governed by official principles (religious in earlier times, both religious and liberal today) in order to cover up actions which are contrary to them—engenders (we saw it again in the case of the war in Algeria) a savory distortion of the vocabulary and thought to which Proust was very attentive. In front of those people who say, because the Princesse de Guermantes is German, because she is a fanatical admirer of Wagner and because her husband has been convinced by the revisionist arguments:

> Every time you come across a Dreyfusard, do a bit of scratching. You'll find that the ghetto, the foreigner, inversion or Wagnermania are not far away.[1]

It is difficult not to recall a phrase used in 1953 or 1954 by a Minister of the Interior which was directed at the parties to the negotiations on Indo-China in whom he stigmatized "the deviation at once intellectual and sexual which passes by Saint-Germain-des-Prés." This "deviation which passes" is an indication that there exist idiocies of language which are the result of the dishonesty, the solecisms of hypocrisy to which one is condemned when one is in the position where one should and should not name a thing, affirm without speaking, promise without committing oneself, and lie nobly. The editorials of Brichot which knock Charlus sideways, the periphrases of M. de

[1] Not in the English version. Pléiade edition, II, p. 1185.

Norpois, the discourses that the narrator's headwaiter delivers to Françoise in order to frighten her, show that, as a result of war, everybody from ministers to valets has gone crazy. Proust places himself at the source where people work out the vocabulary of optimistic views and the mechanics of imposture which are intended to stave off the danger of any rational discussion. And no image is more deserving of being passed on to posterity, as a monument to bourgeois patriotism, than that of Mme Verdurin reading in a newspaper about military operations and the news of the torpedoing of the *Lusitania* while dipping into her café au lait a *croissant* for which, owing to food rationing, she had had to get a prescription from Cottard who had not hesitated to certify that in the circumstances the *croissant* was his patient's only remedy against migraine.

WHAT CAN HAVE LED Proust in spite of his ignorance of sociology and economics (when he and Saint-Loup read Proudhon he sounds like some odd kind of poet) to escape from the pressures at work in, and the blindness of, his milieu? That alone is sufficient to prove that psychological reflection on history, on politicians, on a social class can lead one to truth because in the same way injustice engenders in its authors psychological distortions which the moralist, the memoir-writer, and the novelist at once recognize as such and by means of them they are able to arrive at the causes. But the delicacy necessary for the reconstruction of a collection of historical factors, when one's starting point is the psychology of a society, is something achieved by only a few writers: a Proust, a Montaigne, a La Bruyère, a Flaubert—certainly not a Saint-Simon or a Balzac who on the contrary cling to, or end up by embracing, political opinions which are the exact opposite of those which ought to emerge from their own findings. It is because he needs a moral sensibility, which is not exactly widespread, in order that without possessing any specialized political knowledge, he can take cognizance of injustice when he is one of those who exercise it and when for himself it is no more than something forming part of everyday life.

One does not come to terms with fanaticism—that, finally, is the lesson which in the midst of an epidemic of Barrèsian chauvinism, Proust has to teach us. The trick of the fanatic consists in invoking the respectable nature of the causes that he claims to be serving—the salvation of the people, the greatness of the nation, prosperity, the burial of his own victims—in order to impose silence on those who denounce him precisely on account of the imposture. That is why we should never compromise with justice, or hold back when faced with a lie or make concessions to violence or its part in intolerance. Intolerance by definition never counts on arguments, on "exchanges of ideas," with its adversary in order to impose itself, but on factual situations—the only ones on which it can safely rely and which it can extend. To imagine that if one avoids a conflict, it will calm down of its own accord is to bow down before a need of expansion which by definition is insatiable because it is not founded on right or reason. This naïve tactic is a form of suicide: the prejudiced are never grateful.

IV

For love always hopes that the object which ignited this ardent flame is capable at the same time of extinguishing it.

Lucretius, IV, 1085–86.

Let us no longer mount guard at his door, Aratos, or use our limbs any more; let the morning cock by crowing deliver some one other than ourselves to painful torpors. Let Molon alone, dear friend, lose his breath at this form of gymnastics. For ourselves, let us think of enjoying peace.

Theocritus, Idyll VII, The Thalysia, 133–8.

Chapter IV

LOVE

———

THE BRIEF QUOTATIONS from two poems used as an epigraph for this chapter reveal, in condensed form, the two attitudes which divide the heart of the narrator in *The Captive* and which co-exist in every passion: the desire to become more and more deeply submerged in the passion and the desire to escape from it; the need always to make it more and more the only contact with life and, inversely, the perpetual feeling that it is passion which cuts us off from life and bars us from its simplest pleasures; passion experienced as the highest level of intensity of our sensibility, and though never attained the only true one; and passion felt again as a form of dessication, being cut off from life; blindness to the spectacle of the world and a sense of being carried far away from the pleasures of love itself; passion, finally, conceived as the sole means of appeasing itself and therefore its growth, infinitely desired, as something indispensable, and alternatively the intermittent dream of *dispensing* with passion at a single blow, turning away and like Plato's prisoner escaping from it, not after coming to terms with it, but by making a sudden half-turn and looking towards places from which its object is absent.

But the last temptation is one to which we can only yield in a dream. The sight of the world, the attractive variety of other possible ways of life only appear to make us fall for them, that is to say, at moments when passion is temporarily satisfied and when as a result we are less conscious of our dependence on it. But if life takes us at our word or, what equally happens, if we take ourselves at our word, then we at once find ourselves in a state of torment. We quickly see that passion was not simply the content of our existence, but its condition. Far from depriving ourselves of the charm of this green herb, of this passer-by who casts an eye on us, this exhibition of paintings that every day we put off going to see, of the friend to whom we do not have time to telephone, very much the reverse happens to us when the person whom we love is suddenly taken away from us. We at once perceive that without passion we have at our disposal still fewer things, that it was the sole intermediary between ourselves and the outer world; that it separated us from life in the sense in which the boat on which we find ourselves in the middle of the ocean separates us from the water. When going out with Albertine, Marcel feels that she is becoming a stranger to him, looks on her as an obstacle which is interposed between his desires and a crowd of other beings. They experience one of those moments when two lovers each turn over their thoughts on their own, when each is aware of what the other is doing, and on top of that they turn them over in vain because any translation of their thoughts into action is impossible so long as the passion lasts. Pleasure or simply peace or the need of some sort of activity, caressed in imagination as something forbidden by the other, would be without any attraction unless, in contradictory fashion, the other continued to be associated with it. The appearance on the horizon of the tiniest motive of jealousy, or the departure of Albertine, is sufficient to demonstrate without the slightest delay that there is no question of choice between passion and another way of life, but only between passion and death or madness. (To be sure, experience proves in nearly every case that this "death" or this folly will only be temporary, but it is nonetheless true that, seen from inside the passion, they are the only alternatives.)

That is why being cured of passion is as much an accident as its birth. One can no more emerge from it voluntarily and reasonably than one can manage it by staying there, and fitting it into everyday life. It is rather that life ceases to be everyday life for us because passion is continually forcing on us either repeated crises of separations and reunions, or the abnormal form of sequestration which in *The Captive* always turns out to be insufficiently hermetic. That is why discussions between lovers about themselves are at once unavoidable and sterile: unavoidable because a happy passion is only a passion which has become even more impossible of fulfilment; sterile because they cannot throw light on anything until the passion has vanished, that is to say, the disappearance of the anguish inspired by the possible reactions of the other party. But once the passion has disappeared, which means that the cause of the differences between the lovers has gone as well, there will be nobody left to take an interest in the arguments which in the past had been started by and between two beings who have become strangers to one another. (I shall return to the question in Chapter VI which is devoted to Proust's pessimism.)

"We have great pain in breaking even when we no longer love," said La Rochefoucauld. But when we love, if we break with an extreme facility, we know that the rupture will be unrealizable. Therefore the truth of the matter is that the rupture never takes place. As Proust puts it, with passion the rupture is never in good faith; it is the method, used by the one who takes the pretended initiative, of forcing the other to give a respite to all the problems of her passion or, as people coyly observe, her "relations" with him. And that is done with the object of putting a stop to the slight desire for independence, the cunning little impertinences and the great uneasiness with the idea of giving a "turn to the screw," bringing about a "recovery of control."

PROUST CHOSE THE EASY WAY, which was the opposite of what he did in his critique of snobbery, by choosing in Albertine a person who was basically unfaithful and given to sleeping round. His story would have been even finer if he had shown that the phenomena, on which I have tried to summarize his views, had occurred between faithful lovers.

What doubts about himself, what an urge to present himself continually in the most favorable light, to envisage from the very first moment, even before it comes into being, a passion as it *will be* when it reaches the stage of mutual destruction of the lovers! For in the last resort the narrator of *Remembrance of Things*

Past is always deceived, or dropped. He is in love with Mme de Guermantes before he meets her and of course without his love being returned. Gilberte and Albertine are girls whom he pursues and who run away from him. There is never any question of his growing tired of anybody except when he has been firmly repulsed. Proust is different in one respect from so many other people; he never shows himself as a person who causes suffering to others, who is loved more than he loves. He displays a great humility, a curious absence of self-esteem in so far as he never for a moment suggests that personal charm could of itself remove from his partners the desire to be unfaithful to him. He is still in need of external methods—a disciplinary framework and good policing. They turn out to be entirely useless in practice. The Proustian mistresses, and not only the narrator's, are simply waiting to be left alone for a couple of minutes in order to "get rid of a passing fancy." The moment you turn your back, they vanish into the toilet with the head waiter. Why does Rachel start "making eyes at a young scholar" in a restaurant? Not simply to annoy Saint-Loup, but (as Proust emphasizes) she often does it with the intention of really meeting the unknown person again later on. But why does she do it on *that particular day*, since Saint-Loup is almost never in Paris, except for the fact that the author wants to return and to link everything up with the universal practice of women *making their escape*: behavior which is quite unnecessary in the present instance because it is only on very rare occasions that Rachel finds herself under Saint-Loup's control?

Proust formulates the principle that one always loves without one's love being returned. That is probably the reason why, in spite of the appalling jealousy from which he suffers, his own love never changes to hate; a description of the dynamism of *amour-passion* which for once differs radically from the Racinian pattern. There is one other thing that Proust has described: in love you can never revenge yourself either because in doing so you would ruin yourself or because you no longer have the least desire to do it. It is true that, as a result of his absence of self-esteem, he never feels the need of revenge. For everywhere in

Proust we come across this humility in principle, this basic lack of confidence in himself, this robustly tough attitude which takes for granted that "the women in our lives" can never be anything but prisoners or fugitives while waiting to become indifferent to us.

When they have become indifferent or before our passion starts, it sometimes happens that like Gilberte they "throw themselves at our heads." And apart from *amour-passion*, we ourselves awaken the desires and inclinations, even the beginnings of passion in other people, provided that we do not succumb to it ourselves. Everything turns out as though *amour-passion* at once put the partner to flight, as though passion could only arouse in her non-passion. If one wishes to keep the beloved, it is only out of interest, "benevolence in the most protective sense of the word"—benevolence of the kind that Baron de Charlus displays towards Morel.

THERE IS, TO BE SURE, an element of simplification in this mechanism: when I want you, you don't want me; when you want me, I don't want you. We should probably find some psychological verification of this point in André Roussin or Jean de Létraz. Proust was mistaken in putting forward the view that negation was the only outcome. It is not true that things *always* turn out like that. But according to Proust, even if it is not always like that, it *ought* to be. The real hazard, which is the result of a "coincidence", is that it will turn out differently. The real illusion is that "things will work out" because in essence love, which is said to be shared, in fact continues not to be. It is never anything but a misunderstanding and a lie except perhaps for a very brief moment when, to use an outmoded but exquisite definition of chance, there is the "meeting of two independent series." But Proust differs from Létraz chiefly because the law, which according to him is general, that prompts people to offer themselves to us either too soon or too late and run away when we go after them, is less a matter of circumstance than the fact that it is not at all a question of the same sort of inclination in both cases. If we do not desire a person who appears to offer herself to us, it is precisely because we desire her so little. The same "offer," if the desire became passion, would appear derisory.

The sudden change from the first to the second kind of desire takes place during the celebrated episode of the return by train with Albertine at the end of *Cities of the Plain*. First of all, Albertine is importunate and irritates the narrator; her presence far exceeds his need of her. Then, after the fatal sentence about Mlle Vinteuil, no presence could possibly ever satisfy the passion which explodes. For in fact, in *The Captive*, it is certainly not said that Albertine does not love the narrator. Many lovers would envy them the life they lead. If we place Albertine's infidelities, which are sporadic, beside the complete surrender of her existence, can we say that they are the cause of the narrator's suffering? The fatality which hangs over *The Captive* from the beginning is more essential. The defeat of passion is inevitable: it belongs to its nature. The hunt for and discovery of infidelities is much more an external confirmation. We might say of them, as one says of God and with as many reasons for believing in success, that if they did not exist one would have to invent them. It is not the discovery of the infidelities that brings about the collapse of passion, but a sense of the impossibility of finding happiness in passion, which prompts the search for proofs of infidelity, itself making infidelity inevitable because when it comes to passion who is there who is not unfaithful? The person whom one loves passionately becomes from this very fact unfaithful, always in retreat in face of our madness. |

WHY? Proust has pointed out that we can be conscious of the lack of interest or the beauty of a person, and still love her and above all suffer from her loss because she plays the part of the liaison officer, the hyphen between ourselves and love, gives us access to a life where love exists, a life which love cleanses of all boredom, a life in which, whatever happens, we are never alone or rather we never feel ourselves alone because the essential fact is the continual *possibility* of communicating with somebody and not the fact of always finding ourselves in her company. Sometimes one may even avoid such company, find it importunate. Yet it remains true that in the depths of our being we are constantly attempting to escape from solitude. And it is, indeed, the announcement of an irremediable solitude which with age will bring that day "which is as sad as a winter night," when the narrator has to admit that money alone and not love will provide him with sexual pleasure for a night with beings "whom he will never see again."

Up to that point, it is not because the object is amiable and loved that love exists, but the object is loved *in order that* love may exist. It follows that in Proust love is not an internal autarchic mechanism whose object would only be a pretext, a screen on to which our subjective obsessions are projected. No doubt this form of projection is never absent from love and the face of the passer-by, whom we might perhaps be able to love, and is sometimes no more than "*un espace vide sur lequel jouerait tout au plus le reflet de nos désirs* (an empty space with nothing more upon it than a flickering reflection of our desires)."[1] But at the same time the desire to love is directed straight towards the exterior; it is a sign of the need to escape from oneself notwithstanding the fact that it is directed less to objective "properties", to "qualities" inherent in the object, than the search for something *by means of the object* and beyond it: the fact of being in love with the object and being loved by it. That is why the beloved is always both an absolute, because she is the only means of access to love, and a collaborator whom one distrusts because an empirical and uncertain individual, with her limitations, her outbursts of temper, her falseness, her versatility, eventually her stupidity and weakness, may not be the ideal collaborator, may even be the worst collaborator possible. That is why she inhabits us completely and is at the same time a stranger to us. At the very moment when her loss would make us suffer a thousand deaths, we find ourselves considering her in everyday life with a sardonic eye and noting down with resignation or irritation her incurable banality. Then, when she has ceased to exist as an object of love, the uncertain individual who remains becomes

[1] III, p. 1045; *The Past Recaptured*: p. 270 (RH); p. 469 (C&W).

more distant from us and more indifferent to us than anybody else; we do not even feel for her ultimate destiny the curiosity we feel for our own most distant relations, the vaguest of our friends. It is because our links with the last, however loose they may be, have been established on account of qualities which belong to him independently of his relations with us. The links are therefore the result of sound and lasting reasons, however minor they may be. On the contrary, the individuality which is independent of ourselves to which the loved one returns, collapses for us, when love collapses, into the void.

When Proust receives at Venice the telegram mistakenly signed Albertine, which makes him believe for a moment that she is not dead, he does not feel the least *curiosity* at the prospect of seeing her again, even if it were only for a moment, not because he is afraid of suffering, but out of sheer lack of interest. We are as far away from women whom we no longer love as we are from the dead, as he will repeat in *The Past Recaptured*. Or then, if he wants to see Gilberte again, it is in order to make use of her as a go-between because she can arrange for him to meet girls at her home. This individuality, in fact, in so far as it belongs to a person not loved by us, does not possess, or only does so in exceptional circumstances, any quality which would make us want to see her in preference to thousands of other people. Therefore the only way of ridding ourselves of a passion, even if it were only beginning, does not consist in verifying, in experiencing once again, its intolerable character, but in avoiding all actual contact with the object, in ensuring that it is physically absent even when it is affectively present because the less often it uses that property of its body which acts as a conductor of the sentiment of love, the more rapidly it will lose it. It is the only case in Proust in which time exercises a day to day influence. It is necessary to treasure the time of separation. It is the result of the force of fact and not of reason, or even of feeling, that we cease to love.

Thus the beloved object is not a beloved object, but a means of loving. The Proustian conception of love, in which people have seen a banal skepticism which reduces passion to a fortuitous

psychological phenomenon, is related on the contrary to the
Platonic vision. On one side there are carnal beings who are
numerous and changing; beyond them there is an eternal object
of love which is incorruptible and permanent. But it is only
through the first that we can take cognizance of the second.
"*Chaque sentiment particulier est une partie de l'universel amour* (Each
particular feeling is a tiny fragment of the universal love)."[1] As
in art, the individual object awakens our longing for a durable
and precious reality. Like the three trees at Hudimesnil, it
serves as a gesture of appeal; it is a flash from a kingdom still
buried even more deeply in us than memory; a kingdom that
not even memory can restore to us. Such is the great difference
between the lesson drawn from the impression one gets in front
of the three trees at Hudimesnil and the analyses of the sensa-
tions evoked by the *madeleine* or the unequal paving stones of
the Quai Conti.

But Plato himself believed in the actual existence of a world
which transcended physical beings. Carnal beauty and the
beauty of works of art may fall back into the state of becoming
and into oblivion; they have fulfilled their function as inter-
mediate stages; their fall is the start of the deliverance of the
spirit. In Proust, who does not believe in any form of tran-
scendence, their annihilation is irremediable. This accounts for
the haunting sensation which causes the shadows of love to
dodge in and out among people like the ferret of the song, like
letters of credit which pass from hand to hand and are used to
pay for twenty purchases without anybody ever cashing them
or, owing to lack of provision, being able to cash them.[2] Certain
people, who are responsible for coining the idea of universal
love, possess the same faculty that we find in Plato for suggesting
the taste of an absolute which does not belong to their imperfect
and flighty nature. In reality, they have only themselves to offer,
but at the same time they inspire the desire for much more than
themselves and reveal their inability to satisfy the need which

[1] II, p. 120; *The Guermantes Way*: I, p. 800 (RH); V, p. 158 (C&W).
[2] For a good example of the ferret course, see III, p. 984; *The Past
Recaptured*, p. 221 (RH); p. 385 (C&W).

they arouse. That is why love is identified with suffering. No person is lovable in himself. They are all lovable because they can all inspire the love of a Sovereign Good which surpasses them. But in Proust the Sovereign Good (*le Souverain Bien*) does not exist. With him a meticulously empirical intelligence in the service of a mystical sensibility refuses out of a concern for truth to grant this sensibility the illusory satisfaction which it demands imperiously. It would have been easy to deal differently with things. It would have been easy to write: "You would not seek me if you had not already found me." It would have been easy to hurry along once again and in the wake of so many other people, and either as a philosopher to extract the positive from the negative, knowledge from ignorance, hope from despair; or as an artist to draw from this very despair lovely mirages which can create the lasting illusion that it stands for the opposite of what it really is. He records the contradiction of human life. Where he shows himself skeptical, it is not through insensibility and he does not deny the existence of a need which is impossible to satisfy, but when he feels the need of an absolute joy he does not conclude that the object of this joy is bound to exist under one form or another in order to satisfy us. It emerges that man is tortured by a desire for objects which do not exist. It is like that, and that is all there is to it.

LIFE IS THEREFORE tragic. And the tragic does indeed inhabit *Remembrance of Things Past* where people are too inclined to see a watered down indulgence which though undoubtedly inspired goes too far in the case of slightly artificial, and in any event too subtle, feelings—the luxury product of solitary refinement. Proust put it in this way:

> *La loi cruelle de l'art est que les êtres meurent et que nous-mêmes mourions pour que pousse l'herbe . . . sur laquelle les générations viendront faire gaiement, sans souci de ceux qui dorment en dessous, leur déjeuner sur l'herbe.*
>
> The cruel law of art is that people die and we ourselves die . . . so that the grass may grow . . . so that thither, gaily and without

a thought for those who are sleeping beneath them, future generations may come to enjoy their *déjeuner sur l'herbe*.[1]

The gaiety comes from the fact that Proust does not stylize the tragic, does not isolate it, or confer on it the weight of an explicit theme because once again it would be "doing" metaphysics in the way in which one can stylize anguish, death, the void, and almost make them seem seductive and productive, give them the appearance, by investing them with the form, of being in themselves the solution they demand, but are obviously unable to provide.

Moreover, Proust is sometimes criticized for being too subtle and at other times for being too simplified. He is subtle in the description and narration of "what is happening"—and his pretended "analyses" are often not so much interpretations or explanations, as the prolonging of descriptions and narrations as long as reality continues to offer itself. On the other hand, he simplifies when he sums up an experience, draws a general conclusion about life from it because it is life itself which appears as a simplification and forbids us, unless we decide to play the *bel esprit*, to go beyond the establishment of one or two truths which are obvious but incomprehensible. Now the fact that something can be at the same time obvious and incomprehensible is repugnant to us precisely because it places a brutal obstacle in the way of the exercise of our own subtlety. We need things that are true, but are explained; or alternatively, things which are incomprehensible, but enriched by an infinite number of commentaries. But only to be able to offer a banal commentary (at any rate so far as the content is concerned) on a thing which is incomprehensible is profoundly humiliating to us and we refuse to listen to anybody talking about it. This explains, for example, why Montaigne's ideas on death, which for that matter are the same as those reached by Proust, enjoy so little prestige with the wits.

According to some commentators, the love feeling as presented by Proust is the product of a particular class and a particular period. This is probably accurate when applied to the

[1] III, p. 1038; *The Past Recaptured*: p. 25 (RH); pp. 459–60 (C&W).

forms of gallantry and the expression of emotion belonging to them. But the very fact of passion, as Proust describes it, seems to turn up in all literatures, in all social classes, in the *mœurs* of all peoples or, more exactly, independently of their *mœurs*.

Proustian jealousy, a product of the refinement of the upper middle class at the end of the century? That class would be more likely to deaden and avoid this kind of jealousy which is so common among the uncultivated, the poor and the illiterate. The idea of *amour-maladie* is not something to be associated exclusively with the wealthy aesthetes of the *belle époque*. It is not only in Proust that jealousy is compared to an organic illness like leukemia or tuberculosis.[1] "For by nourishing the abscess it revives and becomes an inveterate illness", said Lucretius. "The pain grows worse if you do not remove the first wounds by fresh ones".[2] These same images, which are to be found in writers using the most diverse aesthetic systems, revolve around the Proustian idea of "the remedy which suspends and aggravates the pain", the idea of the accumulation of the time of separation which the briefest meeting will pulverise.

> *Ma blessure trop vive aussitôt a saigné,*
> My open wound at once poured blood again[3]

says Phèdre. And when Proust compares passion to intoxication, are we not involved with the ancient image of the philtre which was common to Theocritus, Tibullus, the Breton cycle— an image translated into the language of modern physiology by *Remembrance of Things Past* which is a sort of *Tristan and Iseult* revised by Claude Bernard? The organic effect of passion, the agonising oppression of jealousy, are such precise phenomena that physiological metaphors come naturally from the pens of poets in order to describe the presence of this *thing* which is at once alien and glued to us. The image of the cure which is simultaneously desired and feared, necessary and impossible, is in no way the result of Proust's familiarity with medical milieux.

[1] III, p. 644; *The Sweet Cheat Gone*: II, p. 834 (RH); XI, p. 314 (C&W).
[2] *De rerum Natura*, IV, 1068–1070.
[3] *Phèdre*, tr. Cairncross, Act I, scene iii, line 304.

Who has not thought of the first part of *Within a Budding Grove* when reading these lines from Catullus?

> *Difficile est longum subito deponere amorem,*
> *Difficile est . . .*
> *Eripite hanc pestem perniciemque mihi,*
> *Quae mihi subrepens imos, ut torpor, in artus,*
> *Expulsit ex omni pectore laetitias.*

The essential core round which loves that have been lived through make and unmake their halo, that mysterious human being, loved in spite of himself and ourself, interchangeable and yet unchanging; scrutinized as though everything depended on what he is in himself and yet accidental, always the victim of doubt, that doubt which whispers in our ear that any being would have replaced him, if chance had disposed of him and us differently—has this essential core an existence of its own, or does its existence come from an illusion whose seat is inside us?

The narrator of *Remembrance of Things Past* is perpetually oscillating between these two fixed ideas. He usually favors the explanation by illusion, the idea of love finding its source in the state of the person who is in love, but most often he promptly contradicts and then corrects himself, without going as far as to believe that the beloved is in control of a power which is capable in itself of effects that go so far beyond it. Sometimes Proust obliterates the object completely: we do not need it in order to love; we love it perhaps much more during its absence, after its death, when the concern about being or not being repaid is abolished. In the middle of the *Vita Nova*, Dante realises that it is something of a consolation for him to cease hoping without ceasing to love, and inaugurates the "new style" in order to describe the effects of his love on himself while remaining completely independent in relation to the object, without calling for an answer and without the object even having to remain alive— free, in short, to love *infinitely*. Thus to a young man who asked him with surprise whether in his view we should regret the existence of the girl whom we loved, Marcel Proust replied (I am quoting Proust's interlocutor) "that that was a matter of course, that if, instead of receiving the girl's reply, I had learnt that she was dead, I should no doubt have suffered great pain, but should have *avoided the inevitable degradation of my own feelings*".[1] *The Sweet Cheat Gone* demonstrates in effect that the physical annihilation of the object does not immediately annihilate either the dependence of the narrator or his jealousy. The breaking of the link does not take place with greater speed than it would have done under the influence of absence. Nothing enables one to remove the narrator's suffering in a rush, and he suffers in the same way that he would have done if he had been ditched and Albertine were not dead, except that he suffers in a more static fashion.

PROUST SOMETIMES makes love depend on certain properties in the person who is loved, at the same time hastening to add that these properties would not be sufficient in themselves to explain the passion. To tell the truth, if Proust had confined himself to attributing all the causes of love to the lover, his thesis would be a very weak one. It would be the same if he had ascribed them all to the loved one. And the same again if he had declared that love is the result of a balance between or a mixture of the two. But what constitutes the actual subject of his love story is the continual movement from one hypothesis to another: the narrator's doubts and oscillations over the nature and origin of what he feels. Since *Remembrance of Things Past* is not a treatise on passion, but the story of several passions, the contradictions and the unilateral theses that we find in it belong themselves to different moments of the story, to the eternal discourse on love maintained by those who love. The differences of opinion on this score follow the states of the narrator; they themselves form part of the novel. The total skepticism of the phrase at the end of *The Past Recaptured* about love as a "reflection of our desires (*reflet de nos désirs*)," depending on *none* of the characteristics of the loved one (which is obviously untrue) is that of a moribund person in whom "sadness is still dominated by fatigue." It is not the same in *Within a Budding Grove, Cities of the Plain, The Captive*

[1] Emmanuel Berl, *Sylvia* (14th ed.), pp. 153–4. Italics mine.

or even *The Sweet Cheat Gone*. In fact, Proust has drawn a very exact portrait of people who are liable to arouse passion and the characteristics which are common to them (and it may be that skepticism about the well-foundedness of feelings, that quickly become unchangeable, to which they give birth is not perhaps the least active of the elements of love, as it may well be that all the theories of *amour-estime* are no more than defensive justifications destined to create this feeling of doubt).

The precise portrait which emerges from Proust's story is no doubt blurred by the imprecision and the hesitancy of the ideas on the same subject of that particular character in *Remembrance of Things Past* who is the narrator, but it exists nonetheless.

In fact, the sexual desires which carry us towards people follow three separate lines, divide into three categories which may be superimposed on one another and coincide in the same person while preserving their differences. The first is the category of "Baroness Putbus's lady's maid," that is to say, sudden sexual desire in its pure state; the brief liaisons between Albertine and the women in the bathing huts; the narrator's gesture at Doncières when he suddenly puts his arm round the girl who is serving him at table, blows out the candle and slips money into her hand so that she will let him go ahead; "possess Mme de Stermaria on the island in the Bois de Boulogne"; Mlle de l'Orgeville who prostitutes herself in brothels . . . The majority of these women are fantasies because the narrator as good as never succeeds in getting his hands on them. Year after year he evokes "Mme de Putbus's first lady's maid" without being moved even at the very end by the fear that the excellent woman has grown old and experienced since the time of which he is speaking. The attraction of her charming and "very Giorgione" figure defies the years and Mme de Putbus's lady's maid of whom we hear from time to time plays the same part in the erotic order as the *Figaro* article in the literary order with this disadvantage over the latter: that she never puts in an appearance.

The second category is the one that might be called "what attracts (*ce qui plaît*)." It includes, for example, the young "rosy-cheeked Venetian . . . who offered to the delighted eye a whole

range of orange tones," whom the narrator, taking account of
what remains of his fortune, thinks of bringing back to Paris with
him, adding, with that lowdown artistic pretence so common
among the wealthy bourgeois: "*C'était un vrai Titien à acquérir
avant de s'en aller* (It was like acquiring a genuine Titian before
leaving the place)."[1]

Finally, when we come to genuine passion, we find that if
Proust declares with such frequency that it is fortuitous, that it
floats round people before descending on them, it is in order to
bring out more effectively its opposition to the desires and feel-
ings aroused by beings "who attract us." The woman we love is
not simply the one woman from among those we know who
attracts us more than any of the rest, even if we give "attract"
its strongest sense—the adorable charm of the young Venetian.
It does not matter which of our friends is able to understand why
a woman attracts us, but Saint-Loup is shattered and speechless
when the narrator shows him the photo of Albertine in *The
Sweet Cheat Gone*. "It commonly happens that ugly people arouse
a feeling of love which remains inexplicable". It is not that
Albertine was ugly; there was nothing unusual about her; she
was not the person Saint-Loup imagined: the most beautiful of
women who had been chosen with a cool head. Passion is some-
thing different from a super-intense attraction carried to infinity.
The proof lies in the fact that we can only desire to be in love
again if we are still or already in the grip of a passion or its
ramifications, but never at those times when the memory of
having been passionately in love is still further away from us
than the feelings of other men. Only the passion of the present
moment enables us to understand the nature of passion and in
The Sweet Cheat Gone Proust rightly considers that even a vague
and impersonal desire "to have a great love" is a sign that he has
not yet detached himself from the memory of Albertine. Once
it has been dissipated, passion becomes alien to us just as when
it is present in us it makes us alien to pleasure and to agreeable
love affairs. Without being dependent on the qualities in the
sense of "good qualities" of the beloved, it is passion which

[1] III, p. 640; *The Sweet Cheat Gone*: II, p. 832 (RH); XI, p. 309 (C&W).

reveals them to us. Love adds to ordinary life in the sense that it enables us to perceive the true qualities which every being possesses, but which when our attitude is cold are not visible to us. It follows that though entirely selfish, love takes us out of ourselves. But it is not these qualities or grace or physical seductiveness which revive the inclination to love: it is something different.

Before leaving Venice, where the young Venetian girl who attracts him satisfies him completely, the narrator is conscious that for the last time the menacing wings of *amour-passion* are hovering over his shoulders by starting a friendship in the hall of the hotel with a young Austrian woman

> . . . *dont les traits ne ressemblaient pas à ceux d'Albertine mais qui me plaisait par la même fraîcheur de teint, le même regard rieur et léger. Bientôt je sentis que je commençais à lui dire les mêmes choses que je disais au début à Albertine, que je lui dissimulais la même douleur quand elle me disait qu'elle ne me verrait pas le lendemain.*
>
> . . . whose features did not resemble Albertine's, but who attracted me by the same freshness of complection, the same cheerful, smiling expression. I soon felt that I was beginning to say the same sort of things to her that I had started by saying to Albertine, that I was concealing the same pain when she said that she would not be seeing me the next day.

It seems that here the "freshness of complection" has what might be called an atomic force which is superior to the "rosy cheeks" of the young Venetian, and that what had "attracted me" is converted into suffering with alarming rapidity. Why? This is the essential point: she had

> . . . *cet air de franchise aimable qui séduisait tout le monde et qui tenait plus à ce qu'elle ne cherchait nullement à connaître les actions des autres, qui ne l'intéressaient nullement, qu'à avouer les siennes, qu'elle dissimulait au contraire sous les plus puérils mensonges.*
>
> . . . that air of frankness which attracted everybody and was due to the fact that she did not try to find out about other peoples' actions, which did not interest her in the least, so much as to talk about her own, which in fact she concealed by the most puerile of lies.[1]

---

[1] Not included in the English version. See the Pléiade edition, III, p. 649.

The people who attract passion (in the sense in which certain objects attract lightning) are therefore those whom we feel to be independent of us, who conceal themselves from us. They are the "runaways" of whom Albertine is an example; the narcissistic characters whom Freud discusses in his essay *On Narcissism* which appeared in 1914. As in the case of Veblen, no communication, but a simple coincidence of the realities described in almost identical terms by Freud and Proust and more or less at the same time. It is not their only meeting point. In addition to a general affinity of thought there are a number of exact parallels between the two writers which are remarkable. Thus Freud wrote *Mourning and Melancholia* in 1917. *The Sweet Cheat Gone* which is, so to speak, a practical illustration of it, the detailed application of the thing to a concrete case, was worked out at roughly the same time. The coincidences of dates are not all of importance and even if Proust had written *The Sweet Cheat Gone* two years later or if Freud had written *Mourning and Melancholia* three years earlier, the similarity, which occurs at completely different starting points and outside all direct communication, is no less impressive. In the essay on narcissism Freud writes:

> For it seems very evident that another person's narcissism has a great attraction for those who have renounced part of their own narcissism . . . The charm of a child lies to a great extent in his narcissism, his self-contentment and inaccessibility, just as does the charm of certain animals which seem not to concern themselves about us, such as cats . . .

Freud had said a few lines earlier:

> The importance of this type of woman [who only loves in the person with whom she is in love the love he shows for her own ego] for the erotic life of mankind is to be rated very high. Such women have the greatest fascination for men, not only for aesthetic reasons, since as a rule they are the most beautiful, but also because of a combination of interesting psychological factors.[1]

One might risk adding that these psychological factors are obvi-

---

[1] *The Complete Psychological Works of Sigmund Freud*, edited by James Strachey, Volume XIV (London, 1957), p. 89.

ously to be found as much among men as among women; as much among homosexuals as among heterosexuals, and that in consequence all the objections based on the real nature of the exclusively homosexual experience of the author and of the model he used for Albertine seem to me to be relevant to what the narrator has to say about his own brief adventures, about people who merely "attract him," even if they attract him a lot, because in these two categories things happen in fact very differently between homosexuals and between men and women: but these objections lose their point when it is a question of passion, which is always one and the same thing.

Freud and Proust are more or less in agreement in saying that passion is the unlimited weakening of our ego in favor of a narcissistic being, of a "runaway" who only loves in us this very weakening, and then concentrates on increasing the weakening from one day to the next. Passion is therefore objectively fortuitous because the person for whom we are overcome by it possesses, in order to move us, and we possess in order to be moved by her, certain precise dispositions. But in practice passion is fortuitous from the point of view of everyday life because the people are numerous who unite in themselves the characteristics designed to make us love them. Among their number, seen in relation to the duration of an individual life, it is certainly "chance" which decides ("It did not last; she was due to return to Austria . . ."). This explains "the astonishment" caused by the "coincidences" each time that one recomposes in one's memory the recollection of a love affair. And also the "weariness" provoked by the "recomposition" which only ends by making everything still more incomprehensible. From this comes the presentiment of our own death which invades us when we foresee the inevitable death of a passion that occupies us completely at a given moment of life because the passions like ourselves only have a factual existence and once their occupation (in the military sense of the term) is completed, we shall soon be in the position of no longer being able to conceive them or put ourselves in the place of the person who experienced them in ourselves. The recollection of visual impressions—"*Mme Swann sous son ombrelle comme sous le reflet d'un berceau de glycines* (Mme Swann beneath her parasol, as though in the coloured shade of a wistaria bower)"[1]—is more enduring than that of the sufferings of the heart which for the moment were more powerful and drove these visual impressions into the background. It is stimulating to recall that in 1893 the future author of *The Captive* wrote in a review in the *Revue Blanche*:

> *Le retour des romanciers ou de leurs héros sur leurs amours défuntes, si touchant pour le lecteur, est malheureusement bien artificiel.*
>
> The return of novelists or their heroes to their dead loves, which is very touching for the reader, is unfortunately very artificial.

Proust no doubt pushed the picture of the contradictions of love to the point at which it becomes really atrocious in order to demonstrate more clearly that even when the beloved is *also* worthy of being loved, that is not the reason why she is loved, nor for that matter is she loved for the opposite reason. We feel that somebody is running away from us when she appears to be the repository, or the fragment that we see by chance, of a felicity that goes beyond her. The great temptation is always to imagine that this element of "beyondness" is a reality. Proust did not yield to the temptation: passion consists of feeling in the finite an infinite which is simply non-existent.

[1] I, p. 641; *Within a Buddnig Grove*: I, p. 487 (RH); III, p. 306 (C&W).

V

It is likely that the observations that I am about to make have already been formulated, and more than once perhaps. Whether they are new or not is of less concern to me than knowing whether they are true.

JORGE LUIS BORGES

Chapter V

MONTAIGNE AND PROUST

———

O N SEVERAL OCCASIONS in the preceding pages I have
mentioned the name of Montaigne in connection with
Proust. In this chapter I want to show why.

"If he returned among us, he would find himself spurned by
everybody," Gide once said of Montaigne. Like Proust or like
Boileau, Montaigne is an author of whom tradition has formed
a picture which is different from the impression made on us by
an unprejudiced study of his work. Gide is right. Montaigne is
not the soft, debonair humanist that he is always made out to be.
And the traditional portrait is so completely without the striking
features of the original that we are tempted to think that those
who censure it feel the need to defend themselves against it and
against certain findings which are as painful to admit as they
are difficult to forget. In the seventeenth century this defensive
attitude is obvious. Pascal, Arnauld, Nicole and Malebranche,
while continually attacking Montaigne, admire and fear him.
They declare that he is "outdated," *dépassé*, to borrow a modern
expression, but are nevertheless unable to prevent themselves
from talking about him. He is one of those writers (usually the
most complex, the most allusive, the richest, the most impossible
to grasp quickly) of whom we might say that they only exist in
order to become outdated. By decree, the philosophers are
bound to outstrip all the Montaignes between the ages of eight-
een-and-a-half and eighteen-and-nine-months.

The first word that comes to mind about him, when we have
read what the commentators have to say, is nonchalance. Let
us add a few synonyms or analogous terms belonging to the same
moral family: softness, indifference, insensibility, intellectual

laziness, skepticism, facile Epicureanism, superficial philosophi-
cal impressionism, etc. On several occasions Pascal accuses him
of being "lascivious," anticipating those people who in the
twentieth century will treat Freud as a pornographer. It is
carried to such lengths that one is a little surprised to observe the
passion that so many illustrious writers and thinkers have dis-
played in their efforts to flay this licentiousness, to squash this
softness, to barricade themselves against this insensibility, to re-
fute this laziness, to argue against these superficial points of
view. The certificate of insignificance willingly awarded to Mon-
taigne, chiefly by philosophers and religious writers, contrasts
with their inability to abstain from re-condemning him. In fact,
while publicising their disdain for a view of his thought which
has been impoverished in advance, they remain intimidated by
the sight of his work whose merit is more qualitative than theore-
tical and is based as much on the mass and variety of his ob-
servations as on the value of each of them taken separately. In
the case of a number of the censors, we can hardly avoid sus-
pecting a slightly mortifying jealousy of a man in whom they are
conscious of an opening up of sensibility, the range and extent of
life covered by him and a rapidity of comprehension in a man
whose image is perhaps a little too wide to fit into their own
screens. It is easier to forgive an author for not replying to the
questions we ask ourselves than to treat as important those which
do not concern us and which should in reality interest everybody.
It is a proof of our own poverty of thought. Montaigne always
offers us more that he announces. He is one of those writers like
a Freud or a Proust from whom we may always hope for some
unexpected observation, who always fill their nets all the more
abundantly because they do not ask themselves in advance what
principles they are going to rely upon in order to establish a con-
nection between all the material they bring to the surface, or
how they are going to reconcile it with some pre-existing expla-
nation or moral attitude.

SUCH AUTHORS are therefore always coming up against the
hostile attitude of those minds which cling more firmly to

theories and "structures" than to the very substance of reality. But we must also agree that these injections of new substance are rarer in the history of thought than doctrinal changes. The desire to see is less widespread than the desire to foresee; the need to discover rarer than the need to explain. Moreover, it is asserted quite gratuitously that Montaigne is vague—Montaigne who tells us:

> *Tout un jour je contesterai paisiblement, si la conduit du débat se suit avec ordre. Ce n'est pas tant la force et la subtilité que je demande, comme l'ordre.*
> I shall quietly contest a whole day if the conduct of the controversy be followed with order and decorum. It is not force nor subtlety that I so much require, as form and order. [III, 8]

For the rest, considering the state of knowledge during his lifetime, Montaigne's supposed philosophical and scientific inadequacy corresponds to the only rigorous attitude that it was possible to adopt at the time. Montaigne was not living in the nineteenth or even the seventeenth century; he did not have at his disposal a genuine science, but only false philosophies. And all the doctrines to which his "skepticism" is opposed are precisely those which themselves opposed, with all their inertia, the scientific discoveries and the working out of a philosophy that took account of them. To have taken sides with one or other of the dominant philosophies from a simple need to adhere to something would have been to take sides with error, to reinforce one of the obstacles placed in the way of imminent and indispensable intellectual progress.

The last chapter of the *Essays* is called "On Experience." How could Montaigne, at the time when he was writing it, have brought himself closer to the truth to come, given proof of less skepticism than by recommending before Bacon, before Galileo, submission to experience, to evidence, and the study of facts that were opposed, for example, to the Church's ban on dissection which was preventing the development of anatomy? When it came to the theory of knowledge, the information available in his time was such that one could hardly make

progress except by the use of imagination. But one could also do
what Montaigne did, and was the only one to do. For philos-
ophers skepticism means a refusal to believe in any philosophy
which for them is tantamount to not believing in anything at all,
while belief in a false philosophy—a philosophy that one knows
to be false—would be a constructive move. We can read pre-
cisely that in the *Essays*: "*Personne n'est exempt de dire des fadaises,
le malheur est de les dire curieusement* (No man living is free from
speaking foolish things; the ill-luck is to speak them curiously)."
[III, 1]

It was never, in fact, the representatives of genuine know-
ledge who tried to bring a case against Montaigne retrospec-
tively on the grounds of "conceptual inadequacy," but century
after century the people working for the restoration of dogmatic,
moralizing and mystical systems. It is true that with him theory
only takes second place. His aim is not to explain, but to demon-
strate, to become conscious and make people conscious of things;
to make them conscious not of a theory of consciousness, but of
reality. Montaigne is not the anti-philosopher; he is simply and
boldly the a-philosopher.

Malebranche ties himself into knots in picking out contradic-
tions in the *Essays*: real contradictions certainly, or at any rate
in so far as it is real to contradict ourselves by declaring in the
month of August: "It's warm," and in December: "I'm cold."
Montaigne says it over and over again: "*Je ne peins pas l'être.
je peins le passage* (I am not painting the being: I am painting the
passage)." [III, 2)—a sentence in which "paint" is perhaps the
most important word. And again: "*Je n'enseigne point, je raconte*
(I am not teaching; I am relating)."

FROM MONTAIGNE'S "STORY" therefore the fideist commen-
tators—it is really misery that calls out for poorhouses!—
extract declarations of intellectual prudence, present them as
declarations of intellectual indifference, failing to perceive the
demand for certainty and intellectual rigor which finds expres-
sion a thousand times in the *Essays*. Like Proust, Montaigne re-
fuses to indulge in that infantile behavior which on the pretext

that we need objects of certainty, either proceeds to manufacture shams or deny the need.

Of his own accord, Montaigne draws a portrait of himself as indolent and difficult to move. The portrait undoubtedly exists in the book, but it coexists with a different portrait in which, without attempting to harmonise the many contradictory features, Montaigne describes himself as passionate, nervous, anguished, violent, versatile: "*J'ai un agir trépignant où la volonté me charrie; mais cette pointe est ennemie de la persévérance* (I have a most nimble motion where my will doth carry me. But this point is an enemy of persuasion)." [III, 10] A trait which is directly contrary to that of an indolent person for whom the difficulty consists rather in beginning to act, in "getting down" to things, but who later on can act or work for a long time because he does so without great expenditure of energy. In this respect, Proust is different from Montaigne; but in fact the feature which is common to them is that they are both falsely lazy and the eternal nonchalance on which Montaigne prided himself resembles the good-natured jest of Proust's who on the fifteen-thousandth page of his manuscript is seriously engaged in explaining to us that he has abandoned the idea of becoming a writer. In reality, they both reveal the same facility in starting as in going on with their books. Their confession of laziness and incapacity therefore comes from some other source, probably from a need to conjure up the anguish they feel in the face of their work and through imagining that it was something that was bestowed on them by chance, done without their wishing it, in bits and pieces, after a sound official renunciation in advance and a public confession of incapacity. We must not be surprised therefore if we find in Montaigne, as in the narrator of *Remembrance of Things Past*, some very marked signs of a depressive character which is literally on the border between the normal and the pathological and which at times verges on the most serious form of melancholy or obsession:

Quand je suis en mauvais état, je m'acharne au mal; je m'abandonne par désespoir et me laisse aller vers la chute . . . Je m'obstine à l'empirement et ne m'estime plus digne de mon soing.

When I am in a bad state I flesh myself on evil and abandon my-
self through despair, and run to downfall . . . I grow obstinate in
empairing; and esteem myself no more worthy of my care, either
all well or all evil. [III, 9]

The inner tumult rises and accelerates under the influence,
which too easily becomes destructive and devouring, of the
tiresome little troubles of everyday life:

*La tourbe des menus maux offense plus que la violence d'un, pour grand qu'il
soit. A mesure que ces épines domestiques sont drues et déliées, elles nous
mordent plus aigu . . . Je ne suis pas philosophe . . . Depuis que [à
partir du moment où] j'ai le visage tourné vers le chagrin, pour sotte cause
qui m'y ait porté, j'irrite l'humeur de ce côté-là, qui se nourrit après et
s'exaspère.*

A multitude of slender evils offendeth more than the violence of
one alone, how great soever. Even as ordinary thorns, being small
and sharp, prick us more sharply and sans threatening, if on a
sudden we hit upon them. . . I am no Philosopher . . . Since I began
to grow towards peevish age, and by consequence toward froward-
ness . . . whatever fond cause hath brought me to it, I provoke
the humour that way, which afterward by his own motion is
fostered and exasperated [III, 9].

When therefore Montaigne remarks in the same chapter, "*Je
me contente de jouir le monde sans m'en empresser* (I am content
to enjoy the world without putting myself out)," are we to be-
lieve that this attitude is natural and spontaneous? Is it not rather
a precaution on the part of a man who knows that he is quick to
fall apart and therefore makes a continual effort to retain con-
trol over himself or to slow himself down? And when he
writes: "*Je désire mollement ce que je désire et désire peu* (What I
wish for I commonly desire the same but mildly, and desire but
little)," we are inclined to see behind this statement an uneasy
person who remains on the alert and who being too knowing to
be vulnerable is afraid of giving himself away. For the same
reason, the deliberate sluggishness is difficult to reconcile with the
bombshell that the death of La Botéie was for him, and above all
with the fact that the interior death, which was what that death
amounted to for the survivor, was fought not by wisdom, but by

another expenditure of emotion: "*L'amour me soulagea du mal qui m'était causé par l'amitié* (Love discharged and diverted me from the inconvenience which goodwill and amity had caused in me)." [III, 4]

We know to what species those people belong who are obliged, in order to stand up to suffering, to resist it not by detachment, but by matching one feeling against another. For the rest, the same man who desires "mildly" and "little" has this to say of love:

> *Je n'ai point d'autre passion qui me tienne en haleine. Ce que l'avarice, l'ambition, les querelles, les procès font à l'endroit des autres qui, comme moy, n'ont point de vacation assignée, l'amour le ferait plus commodément : il me rendrait la vigilance, la sobriété, la grâce, le soing de ma personne, r'assurerait ma contenance à ce que les grimaces de la vieillesse, ces grimaces difformes et pitoyables, ne vinssent à la corrompre ; me remettrait aux études sains et sages, par où je me pense rendre plus estimé et plus aimé, ôtant à mon esprit le désespoir de soy et de son usage et le raccointant à soy.*
>
> I have no other passion that keeps me in breath. What avarice, ambition, quarrels, suits in law, or other contentions work and effect in others who as myself have no assigned vacation or certain leisure, love would perform commodiously: it would restore me the vigilancy, sobriety, grace and care of my person; and assure my countenance against the wrinkled frowns of age (those deformed and wretched frowns) which else would blemish and deface the same; reduce me to serious, to sound and wise studies, whereby I might procure more love, and purchase more estimation: it would purge my mind from despair of itself, and of its use, acquainting the same again with itself. [III, 5]

Thus love is not only for him the one spur to activity, the force which will sustain him and help him to grow old well, but is the only interior climate which is completely favorable to intellectual work.

We could repolish a good many other mirrors in which are reflected Montaigne's desperate emotionalism, his vulnerability, his instability, his anxiety; all of them visible, for example, in his need to travel and not simply in search of cures at watering places or for the purpose of instruction but, as he expressly says, in order to escape the tension which quickly becomes unbearable

for him and unreasonably exhausting, as well as from the daily
occupations which "devour" him.

On the other hand, Montaigne tells us precisely what he is by
nature and principle: violent and crushing in conversation:

> *Je hais à mort de sentir au flatteur . . .*

("*Je hais à mort*"—I deadly hate—what language for a noncha-
lant person!)

> . . . *Je me jette naturellement à un parler sec, rond et dru, qui tire, à qui ne
> me connait d'ailleurs, un peu vers le dédaigneux.*
>
> . . . which is the cause I naturally affect a pithy, sinewy, dry,
> round, and harsh kind of speech; which of such as have no further
> acquaintance with me, is judged to incline to disdain. [I, 40]

This talk sometimes carries him so far that he describes himself
in these terms (in the rest of the passage quoted above: "I shall
quietly contest a whole day, if the conduct of the controversy
be followed with order and decorum"):

> *Mais quand la dispute est trouble et déréglée, je quitte la chose et m'attache
> à la forme avec despit et indiscrétion, et je me jette à une façon de debattre
> testue, malicieuse et impérieuse, dequoy j'ai à rougir après.*
>
> But when the disputation is confounded and orderless, I quit the
> matter and betake me to the form, with spite and indiscretion,
> and embrace a kind of debating, testy, headlong, malicious and
> imperious, whereat I afterwards blush. [III, 8]

Montaigne is therefore someone who is living perpetually under
the threat of emptying himself at a single blow of all his
energy, whether in solitary rumination on obsessive subjects or
in the contrariness of bad exchanges with other people. Our
apathetic humanist never departs from his conversational style
even in his relations with his mistresses. An epicurean façade is
pierced by a jealous violence; behind the mask of a Philinte
there is an Alceste who is completely caught up by the fatal
eccentricity of wanting to correct and amend the women he
loves:

> *De colère et d'impatience un peu indiscrète, sur le point de leurs ruses et
> desfuites et de nos contestations, je leur en ai fait voir parfois: car, je suis,*

de ma complexion, sujet à des émotions brusques, qui nuisent souvent à mes
marchés, quoiqu'elles soient légères et courtes. Si elles ont voulu essayer la
liberté de mon jugement, je ne me suis pas feint à leur donner des avis
paternels et mordants, et à les pincer où il leur cuisait.

I have sometimes given them a taste of choller and indiscrete im-
patience, upon occasions of their wiles, sleights, close-conveyances,
controversies and contestations between us; for, by complexion, I
am subject to hasty and rash motions, which often impeach my
traffic, and mar my bargains, though but mean and of small worth.
Have they desired to essay the liberty of my judgements, I have
never disembled to give them fatherly counsel and biting advice,
and showed myself ready to scratch them where they itched. [III,
5]

This intransigent sincerity is not the result of misanthropy though
it can lead to it. On the contrary, it supposes an intensive need
of friendly relations and intelligent exchanges—a need so in-
tense that, as he assures us, he would have preferred to confide
his ideas to an interlocutor rather than write them down him-
self, if he had been able to find one after the death of La Boétie:
"*Je suis tout au dehors et à l'évidence, né à la société et à l'amitié* (I am
all outward in appearance; born for society and unto friend-
ship)." [III, 3] Montaigne differs from Rousseau in that he does
not seek isolation, but submits to it. His moods, the animation
of his intelligence, are directly tributory to the company he
keeps:

> *Comme notre esprit se fortifie par la communication des esprits vigoureux et*
> *réglés il ne peut dire combien il perd et s'abâtardit par le continuel com-*
> *merce et fréquentation que nous avons avec les esprits bas et maladifs.*
> But as our mind is fortified by the communication of regular and
> vigorous spirits, it cannot well be expressed how much it loseth
> and is bastardised by the continual commerce and frequentation
> we have with base, weak and dull spirits. [III, 8]

It is to Montaigne that we owe the first and finest of those
writings on the spirit of conversation which occupy such a large
place in our literature and in spite of that have introduced some
rare fruits into our manners. For the man whom Pascal de-
scribes as "the admirable author of 'The Art of Conferring'"

friendship is, contrary to what it is for Proust, a means of getting to know oneself; and if he says, as Proust does less concisely, "We must lend ourselves to others, but only give us to ourselves", he is thinking, as he emphasizes, not of friendship but of purely social contacts, of engagements entered into with people of important positions, holding responsibilities and careers.

MONTAIGNE AND PROUST know human nature because they are in themselves several different men, because there are few human feelings, already existing in embryo in themselves, that they cannot experience if they set out to do so. They have that spider's web kind of sensibility which enables them to penetrate another person's defences and discover exactly how he feels. It is a polymorphous sensibility which is the only true source of ideas in psychology, but which, in those who possess it, makes the acquisition of a personal equilibrium a difficult and always precarious business. Or rather, the equilibrium is constantly being broken from day to day, but the continuous rupture is simply the raw material of a general equilibrium extending over the whole of existence. We might say of both of them that out of days as psychopaths they constructed the lives of sages.

Neither of them is a misanthrope, but both are pessimists. Montaigne admits that, when reading historical works, he instinctively goes for everything which lowers mankind, for dark authors like Tacitus. But except in his relations with his mistresses, Montaigne belongs more to the race of the Philintes than the Alcestes: inclined to pessimism, but loving mankind.

WHY, THEN, DID THE MAN who often speaks of the frankness of his approach, his propositions, his open countenance, his air of truth, the naturalness of his expression, the man who inspires sufficient confidence and sympathy, simply by the grace with which he received them, to discourage attacks on him by the bandits who had come to kill him and pillage his house—why did this man also write "On Solitude" and live so much alone?

It was not a matter of taste or inclination or mood: it was

because of his horror of injustice. Montaigne hates violence and cruelty; he flays them everywhere and devotes an entire essay to an indictment of them (II, 11). He also wrote what from the moral and psychological points of view ranks as one of the most vigorous and intelligent attacks in the whole of our literature on torture (II, 5). Now he considers that he is living in an age when, owing to the Wars of Religion and the discovery of the New World, it is impossible to manage public affairs, to take part in social life, and almost impossible to walk out of one's house without becoming closely or distantly involved in collective crime. It is because for Montaigne, as it was to be later for Rousseau and Kant, no interest can or should interfere with a complete respect for justice:

> La justice en soy, naturelle et universelle, est autrement réglée, et plus noblement, que n'est cette autre justice speciale, nationale, contrainte au besoing de nos polices.
>
> Justice in itself natural and universal is otherwise ordered, and more nobly distributed, than this other especial and national justice, restrained and suited to the need of our policy. [III, 1]

But force is disguised as law. The moral conscience is weakened to the extent of regarding cruelty as something normal:

> Je vis en une saison en laquelle nous foisonnons en exemples incroyables de ce vice, par la licence de nos guerres civiles; et ne voit-on rien aux histoires anciennes de plus extrême que ce que nous en essayons tous les jours. Mais cela ne m'y a nullement apprivoisé. A peine me pouvais-je persuader, avant que je l'eusse vu, qu'il se fût trouvé des âmes si monstrueuses, qui, pour le seul plaisir du meurtre, le voulussent commettre . . .
>
> I live in an age wherein we abound with incredible examples of this vice, through the licentiousness of our civil and intestine wars; and read all ancient stories, be they never so tragical, you shall find none to equal those we daily see practised. But that hath nothing made me acquainted with it. I could hardly be persuaded before I had seen it, that the whole world could have afforded so marble-hearted and savage-minded men, that for the only pleasure of murder would commit it . . .

How long shall we have to wait after Montaigne to find this kind of courage in a writer? The few prudent and invariably

vague allusions to politics and violence that we find in seven-
teenth-century writers are lame compared with the forthright-
ness with which the *Essays* go straight to the facts, never recoiling
when faced with the need to be precise, to give details, to men-
tion circumstances, and to call things by their names. Then again,
when people speak of Montaigne's conservatism, they are only
taking into account a part of his writings, are forgetting the un-
equivocal way in which he adopted a firm attitude to so many
actual problems and public evils from which his age suffered:
the vices of the judicial institutions, war, religious intolerance,
the conquest of the American peoples. It would be necessary to
quote in their entirety the pages in which he denounces the use
of European "methods" in America: "Our world has just dis-
covered another" etc. (III, 6). Could he have formulated a more
severe condemnation of Christian civilization than his declara-
tion, made perhaps too optimistically, that the pagans would
have behaved more morally and more humanly than ourselves?

> *Que n'est tombée sous Alexandre ou sous ces anciens Grecs et Romains une
> si noble conquête . . . Au rebours, nous nous sommes servis de leur [aux
> Indiens] ignorance et inexpérience à les plier plus facilement vers la
> trahison, luxure, avarice, et vers toute sorte d'inhumanité et de cruauté à
> l'exemple et patron de nos moeurs. Qui mit jamais à tel prix le service de la
> mercadence et de la trafique?*
>
> Why did not so glorious a conquest happen under Alexander, or
> during the time of the ancient Greeks and Romans? . . . Whereas,
> contrariwise, we have made use of their ignorance and inexperi-
> ence to draw them [the Indians] more easily into treason, fraud,
> luxury, avarice and all manner of inhumanity and cruelty, by the
> example of our life and the pattern of our customs. Who ever
> raised the service of merchandise and benefit of traffic to so high
> a rate?

And in the recent post-war epoch, when for some fifteen years
France's main occupation was a series of attempts to impose her-
self by force of arms and without quarter on peoples who were
weaker and much more wretched than herself, is it possible for a
Frenchman who is still a man to read without a terrible sadness
this final sentence of a splendid act of accusation written four
centuries ago?

Tant de villes rasées, tant de nations exterminées, tant de millions de peuples passés au fil de l'épée, et la plus riche et belle partie du monde bouleversée pour la négociation des perles et du poivre.

So many goodly cities ransacked and razed, so many nations destroyed and made desolate, so infinite millions of harmless people of all sexes, states and ages, massacred, ravaged and put to the sword; and the richest, the fairest and the best part of the world topsiturvied, ruined and defaced for the traffic of Pearls and Pepper. [III, 6]

It follows that Montaigne's "conservative" propositions ("Of Custom, and how a Received Law should not easily be Changed") are only conservative in their own special way. It is sufficient to remember that his pages against sedition refer to the Wars of Religion and their massacres, that a refusal to subscribe to the Catholic *and* the Protestant causes was the most progressive position one could possibly adopt in the sixteenth century, and that Montaigne's consistent attitude during the wars was like that of the author of *The Past Recaptured* during the war of 1914–1918: an inflexible resistance to the eye-wash which completely blotted out all morality and reason; the preservation of a meritorious clear-sightedness in the midst of a vortex and the demands of fanaticisms which were a mixture of complicity and opposition. Montaigne's resistance, indeed, is extraordinarily vehement. We are surprised, for example, to find that his intolerance in military matters is expressed in words (they refer to Caesar) as strong as those in which he chose to denounce "*les fausses couleurs dont il veut couvrir sa mauvaise cause et l'ordure de sa pestilente ambition* (the false colours wherewith he goeth about to cloak his bad cause, and the corruption and filthiness of his pestilent ambition)." [II, 10]

We should be glad to see a writer appear in France today who was as widely read as Montaigne was in his lifetime and who shouldered his responsibilities with the same clear-sightedness— I mean the way in which his responsibilities form part of the substance of his work instead of being treated incidentally, as though he were simply a Mr. X—criticising and attacking the injustices, the vices, the stupidities, the abuses, the social, intellectual, political, moral, philosophical and religious errors. It is a curious thing, this myth of Montaigne as an "uncommitted" writer, and this harking back to his supposedly conservative theories because it is not difficult to understand that to say at that time, "All institutions, all religions are of equal value" was tantamount to saying that, in fact, none of them was worth anything, that it led to the proscribing of intolerance and to the statement of the principle that no institution, no religion should be imposed by force in place of others. It is a strange kind of support for accepted beliefs to assert coldly that, if one must submit to the laws of one's country, it is in no sense because they are just, but because one is accustomed to doing so! Pascal saw the danger when anxious to prove that, once they are perceived, the absurdity and injustice of human affairs lead to a revival of Faith and not to practical improvements, and replied:

> *Montaigne a tort . . . Le peuple suit [la coutume] par cette seule raison qu'il la croit juste. Sinon, il ne la suivrait plus . . . Il y obéit [aux lois], mais il est sujet à se révolter dès qu'on lui montre qu'elles ne valent rien.*
> Montaigne is wrong . . . The people follow custom solely because they believe that it is just. Otherwise, they would not follow it any longer . . . They obey the laws, but they are liable to revolt as soon as some one shows them that the law and custom are worth nothing.

Pascal is therefore advocating by implication a State founded on lies in which only a minority has the privilege of knowing that custom supports institutions which are always bad by assuming the right to tell people that the laws are just.

Yet for Montaigne, laws, even if they are bad ones, are always preferable to the absence of law. Language which would appear in bad taste in contemporary Paris of 1960, where personal power sets itself above the laws that it has itself enacted in accordance with its own convenience, and where French intellectuals see five centuries of political thought culminating in the beatitude which they derive from the contemplation of a sort of Liberal Empire which in any case is growing less and less liberal. It is sounder to refer to a sixteenth-century author if one wants to hear somebody assert, without ambiguity or any consideration for rank, that a respect for the laws, whatever they may be, is always preferable to protection which depends on the benevolence of individuals. Montaigne loathes the idea of subjection to great men. He writes: "*Me déplaît être hors la protection des lois et sous autres sauvegardes que la leur* (It displeases me to be outside the protection of the law and under some other safeguard than that)." [III, 9] He realises, however, that the law has become a mask for injustice.

> *Pareilles consciences logent sous diverses sortes de robe, pareille cruauté, déloyauté, volerie; et d'autant pire qu'elle est plus lâche, plus sûre et plus obscure sous l'ombre des lois.*
>
> The same consciences are to be found under different garbs; the same cruelty, the same disloyalty, the same thieving; all the worse because it is more cowardly, more secure and more hidden under the shadow of the law. [III, 9]

The supposed legality is simply a farce. The virtues of public men are only virtues in the sense of being "on show," and in this way, in such a century, "the favourable views of the people [= public opinion in general] is harmful" [III, 2]. It is all very simple. There are periods when to be regarded as a person of integrity or, more important still, as a person who has won fame, means to dishonor oneself morally. For this reason Montaigne detaches himself from the society of his time and takes shelter on his own, having seen what one must do and keep quiet about in order, as we say today, to "be a success." "*Répondons à l'ambition que c'est elle-même qui nous donne le goût de la solitude* (Let us reply to ambition that it is itself the thing which gives us a taste for isolation." [I, 39]

It will no doubt be said that this is a retreat into subjectivity, a flight towards the mirage of the *belle âme.* Now it is exactly the reverse of that. How many writers and philosophers coming after him have shown as little hesitation as Montaigne over compromising themselves? Think of the flattery of Descartes and Pascal when writing to the great.

We should be circumspect about the passages in which we think that we are coming across Montaigne's "mediocre" ideal. When he says, for example, "*Je me contente . . . de vivre une vie seulement excusable* (I am well pleased . . . to live a life that is

only excusable),'' [III, 9] we must remember that according to
him nothing is more difficult than to live a life which is "only
excusable" because in his eyes the majority of men are in fact
"inexcusable," at any rate in so far as they are members of a
civilization. It is one of Proust's most firmly held ideas that par-
ticipation in a "collective crime" is unforgivable. Although
highly responsible in their role as social beings, men are never
guilty—for there they are what they are—in their "private"
lives. Here Montaigne the pre-psychoanalyst substitutes himself
for the political moralist in order to insist that men never suffer
remorse when they ought to do so—as a result of public in-
justices, for example—but against this are tormented when they
have no reason to feel remorse—in their sexual life, for example.
"*Que fait l'action génitale aux hommes . . . Pour n'en oser parler . . .
Nous prononçons hardiment: tuer, dérober, trahir* (Why was the act of
generation made so natural to men . . . seeing we fear to speak
of it . . . we pronounce boldly to rob, to murder, to betray)."
Montaigne's hesitation does not extend, as we can see, to moral
judgements and if, when it is a question of describing the
hypocrisy of his fellow men, he weighs his words, it is not
without having chosen them:

> *Ils envoient leur conscience au bordel et tiennent leur contenance en règle.
> Jusques aux traîtres et assassins, ils épousent les loix de la cérémonie et
> attachent là leur devoir.*
>
> They send their conscience to the stews, and keep their counten-
> ance in order. Even traitors and murderers observe the laws of
> complement, and thereto fix their endeavours. [III, 5]

The long essay called "On Some Verses of Virgil" is not new
simply "for the period." One would have preferred him to call
it "On Some Verses of Lucretius," and for the center round
which the essay proliferates to have been a quotation from Book
IV of *De Rerum Natura* because in a general way Lucretius was
far more estimable and far greater than the celebrant of the
moral order and the return to earth, the starchy laureate of
Work, the Family, and the Fatherland. Moreover, in Virgil's
lines it is a question of a married couple and Montaigne does not

fail to comment in this way on the intensity of feeling with which the poet invests the conjugal moment: "He depainteth her somewhat stirring for a marital Venus."

In this essay Montaigne, who was not exactly "marital" himself, succeeds in speaking about physical love without making the least concession either to ribald convention or prudishness. The seventeenth century was prudish and we have seen that Pascal reproached him for using "lascivious" words. On the other hand, libertinage will be emancipation for a sexuality which was still considered a taboo and which in consequence people *enjoyed* transgressing. For Montaigne sexuality is neither fun nor immodest; it is simply a fact of life. He was the first—and for a long time the only—person who succeeded in talking about it without circumlocutions or provocation.

There is one other way in which Montaigne is original. When he writes about love, he does so from the woman's point of view and not merely from the man's. He rejects the fiction that society is ruled by and for men. According to that view, sexuality would be less important for women than for men. It is a principle, as we know, which was the basis of the sexual morality (formulated and set up as a model in *La Nouvelle Héloïse*) of the bourgeoisie in the nineteenth century for whom frigidity, even in marriage, was one of the essential attributes of the decent woman, while husbands had the right to diverge: "*Je dis que les masles et les femelles sont jetés en même moule. Sauf l'institution et l'usage, la différence n'y est pas grande* (I say that both male and female are cast in the same mould; instruction and custom excepted, there is no great difference between them)." In saying this, he shows clearly, on the one hand, that he has grasped the Freudian fact about the identity and the equality of the libido in both sexes which differs only in the matter of anatomy and education. On the other hand, there is the link which exists in our societies between the failure to understand the feminine libido and the practical and legal subordination of women to men. And he adds: "*Platon appelle indifféremment les uns et les autres (les masles et femelles) à la société de tous estudes, charges, exercices, vacations guerrières et paisibles, en sa république* (Plato calleth them both

indifferently to the Society of all studies, exercises, charges and
functions of war and peace in his Commonwealth)." [III,
5]

Such liberty, which is completely free from any licentious
undertone, as well as any element of censure is only conceivable
in regard to a problem of this nature because it forms part of a
coherent attitude to things as a whole. It is the attitude dis-
played by Montaigne all through the *Essays*. It is a sort of dis-
cipline of relaxation: a continual fidelity to the thought which
emerges—an immediate response and adherence to the mood
actually experienced—and not to a mood that one ought, that
one would like, or is supposed to experience. It is a discipline
which produces the literary work that comes closest to the spirit
of Freudian analysis before the time of Proust. Indeed, for
Montaigne, as for Proust, it is not a matter of constructing a
vision of man, but of seeing him, and for this reason of *pushing on
one side the obstacles which prevent one from seeing him*. That is why he
is unpopular with the dogmatists. His line is first to put a stop to
the desire to explain, to judge, to understand things too quickly.
He adopts it in order to allow the psycho-physiological event to
reach its proper level and give it time to free itself, so that he can
listen to it in a way which reduces distortion to a minimum.
Next it reduces to a minimum the need to justify or accuse one-
self, the rush to bring the least discovery or admission before a
moral tribunal. For this need obviously puts a limit on the ex-
tent of the discoveries. It requires vigilance to *enable oneself to
arrive* in the manner in which Proust, too, brings it off in *The
Sweet Cheat Gone*, and to give the lead to the interest of pronounc-
ing on the mania for classification. The abundance like the
variety of Montaigne's "story" comes from the fact that he has
managed to extricate himself from the haunting sense of guilt.
While St. Augustine and Rousseau write *Confessions*, pride them-
selves on admitting their "turpitudes," and assemble the material
for a lawsuit in which, in the dual capacity of judges and liti-
gants, they take it in turns (like Courtelines' Barbemolle in *Un
Client sérieux*) to put the case for the prosecution and the case for
the defence, Montaigne calmly maintains that he does not see in

whose name he could legitimately condemn himself, at any rate in his private and not his public life:

> *Quant à moy, je puis désirer en général être autre; je puis condamner et me déplaire de ma forme universelle, et supplier Dieu pour mon entière réformation et pour l'excuse de ma faibless naturelle. Mais cela, je ne le puis nommer repentir, ce me semble, non plus que le déplaisir de n'être ni ange ni Caton. Mes actions sont réglées et conformes à ce que je suis et à ma condition. Je ne puis faire mieux . . . Si d'imaginer et désirer un agir plus noble que le nôtre produisait la repentance du nôtre, nous aurions à nous repentir de nos opérations les plus innocentes.*

> For my part, I may in general wish to be other than I am; I may condemn and mislike my universal form, I may beseech God to grant me an undefiled reformation, and excuse my natural weakness: but meseemeth I ought not to term this repentance, no more than the displeasure of being neither Angel nor Cato. My actions are squared to what I am and confirmed to my condition. I cannot do better . . . If to suppose and wish a more nobler working than ours, might produce the repentance of our own, we should then repent of our most innocent actions. [III, 2]

We can see that the disclaimer of pathological guilt (think of Freud, think of the super-ego torturing the ego as a punishment for what are in fact its "most innocent actions") would have appeared undesirable to Pascal because it strikes at the root of the principle of the "imperfection" of human nature and removes the weapon which is essential to moral terrorism. There is no question in the *Essays* of preaching *self-indulgence*, as the Christian moralists of the seventeenth century were only too prone to argue. Montaigne shows no indulgence for the faults and the crimes *that we are in a position to prevent*: the crimes whose victims are man and humanity in the name of the interest or the *raison d'Etat*, or of intolerance. Man commits crimes against his fellow men; he is never in a state of sin in himself. There are actions which are good or bad, beneficial or harmful; and evil means criminal, but never natural actions.

Thus Montaigne succeeds in writing a book about himself while at the same time liberating himself from two contradictory needs which are both equally strong and equally widespread: the need to justify one's existence at any price—and to declare oneself dissatisfied with it. Normally, when we talk about ourselves, we try to prove at the same time that nobody could have done better in the position in which we were placed, and that we are intrinsically superior to the result obtained. Montaigne does not accept either of these two forms of consolation.

Does he in any case write all that much about himself? It is standard practice to oppose Pascal's sentence about the "stupid plan" to paint one's own portrait by the one from the *Essays* on "*la forme entière de l'humaine condition* (the human condition in its entirety)". More simply, we might say that Montaigne writes at least as often, if not more often, about things outside him as about himself. When many writers like Chateaubriand, for example, while pretending to talk about nature, a political situation, a conversation with a great man, a foreign country, are only talking in reality about themselves and cannot avoid returning to a self which in any case varies very little, Montaigne, who is always saying that he wants to talk about himself, turns out a few lines later to be talking about Italy, Tacitus, politics, cooking, medicine, or domestic economy. It is less himself that he paints than the variety of his reactions to the real world and he therefore paints the real world. It is less often his conscience than the things of which he is conscious. He differs from so many other writers who use the world as a pretext for talking about themselves while he uses himself as a pretext for talking about the world. What is more, if he talks about himself, it is not because he regards himself as an exceptional person; he is not telling the story of a "destiny"—less even than Proust—and his tone always remains modest without its being necessary for him to keep a watch over himself in order to ensure that it is so. For the rest, in spite of the fact that they both have their official position in an ego, neither the *Essays* nor *Remembrance of Things Past* really belongs to the literature of confession. They never have the confidential tone that a Chateaubriand adopts with the consciousness of revealing a sublime "interior," hidden until then from the eyes of mortals. The two writers on the ego are modest; they are not egocentric, but for most of the time might be described as "egofuge."

BOTH BEFORE AND AFTER Montaigne, the rare psychological observations forming part of the content of literature, as of philosophy, are all subordinated to the intention of formulating a way of life. It is a psychology of directors of conscience. It is always a matter of preferring some things to others, of teaching people to despise a whole area of human existence, which is of course something that can be done convincingly with the help of exact observation. But by dividing man between strength and weakness, we are prevented from describing him realistically because the knowledge of fact falls short of what is necessary in favour of a judgement of value.

Lastly, from Montaigne we learn that it is not a fault to feel sleepy, to desire, to prefer some foods to others, to be dreamy, to forget, to be afraid, to fear death, to develop habits, to be lazy, to hate illness, to waste one's time, to be morose or sad, to suffer and to be joyful. And we not only learn that such things are not faults; we also learn that the supposed weaknesses are linked to "strengths" of which they may be the condition, that there are in fact neither strengths nor weaknesses, and that it is in vain, as Freud well demonstrated from experience, to repudiate a part of ourselves as though it were a stranger to us. Even today the philosophers with their hankering after the "authentic" and the unauthentic in man, hasten to instal, metaphorically speaking, in the heart of the human being this eternal lawsuit. But in man there are not some things that are important and others that are not, a noble and a trivial sector, the authentic and the unauthentic: man behaves in the same way in great matters and in small. And taking cognizance of the fact does not mean for Montaigne that one is authorised to renounce all moral judgements on oneself. That, indeed, is where the error of Pascalian criticism lies. Montaigne's demands, chiefly in matters of justice and truth, are very precise and cannot be satisfied by false appearances. For example, the moral quality to which Montaigne attaches perhaps the greatest importance is the one that affects the others: loyalty. His horror of lying is absolute, truly Kantian before Kant. So, too, is his definition of morality, his principle that it must be cultivated for its own sake and not on account of

the advantages or the consideration that it brings us. Montaigne
is therefore no more of a skeptic in morality than in philosophy.
By refusing to submit to moral judgement factors which do not
derive from it, but from the diversity of prejudices, fanaticisms,
the practices and beliefs of different societies, he does not destroy
morality; he makes it possible. Responsibility begins when ac-
tions begin, whether personal or political, which can affect
other people, in spite of the fact that I myself am not guilty of
being and I alone know whether I am "cowardly or courageous."

If one wanted to oppose Montaigne in summary fashion to his
greatest admirer and principal adversary, Pascal, one might say:
for Pascal I am guilty when I feel a personal desire for happi-
ness—in front of a beloved, a glass of wine, a comfortable bed-
room, a beautiful landscape—but I am not bound to worry
about impostures, hetacombs, or the injustices which surround
me. For Montaigne the position is exactly the reverse.

THE RELATIONSHIP between Montaigne and Proust is per-
haps the result of keeping at a distance the feeling of patholog-
ical guilt: an elimination which permits their "story" of man to
flow and spread in all its breadth without his being haunted by
the fear that he has to render an account at every moment. And
if Montaigne is such a great writer—greater even than Proust—
it is perhaps partly because he is still freer than Proust from feel-
ings of pathological guilt, while Proust's feeling of guilt is pro-
jected in its entirety into his "remorse at not writing," and sub-
sists therefore in this particular domain although all the rest of
the Proustian territory has been liberated from it. Their rela-
tionship is also due to a determination to give a good reception
to everything that happens in and around them by abstaining
from instantaneously awarding a mark to each thing—a coeffi-
cient of importance. That is why we find in the *Essays*, as in
Remembrance of Things Past, numerous observations which by
their content are situated on the fringe or even in the interior of
psychoanalysis. *Remembrance of Things Past* can be read exactly as
though it were a "psychopathology of everyday life." Another
example: Proust finishes like Freud by seeing in a certain form

of amorous passion the inevitable *repetition* of a rigid but still active past, by seeing therefore in passion the incorporation of that past into a present situation which is variable, but in face of which we cannot invent a fresh solution. Like Freud he attributes to this factor the development of the jealousy without issue that results from it; then the brutal elimination of the affectivity that follows when passion ceases and interest in the object ceases too.[1]

Montaigne also frequently takes note of phenomena whose reality even Freud's contemporaries would find difficulty in admitting: for example, in the passage in Book II, chapter I, where he describes the sado-masochistic components which are part of all human psychism.

The reason for these particular discoveries is to be found in the general attitude which is common to Proust and Montaigne. It is in fact a characteristic of all works which from an intellectual, as from a moral point of view, are liberating, to show the influence on man of motives of action other than those he attributes to himself, and different from the principles which he believes in good faith to be his. This type of comprehension can be found in Montaigne, La Rochefoucauld or Proust. The conscious activity is presented in their case as a simple projection or justification of an affectivity whose genesis is unconscious and, according to them, no aspect of man should be regarded as more moral, more noble than another aspect or another "part" of the personality. There are only *events*, which should be judged according to the effective part they play in the history of the individual and not according to a scale of values which could only be worked out precisely by the function justifying, excusing and magnifying man. The essence of this attitude is always to give priority to content over form, to the thing over the sign which gives it its name, to the cause over the pretext. And the periodical reaction against this attitude consists in the inverse

---

[1] Another psychoanalytical premonition is this sentence about homosexuals: they "*consomment dans leur visage la profanation de leur mère* (consummate upon their faces the profanation of their mothers)." II, p. 908; *Cities of the Plain*: II, p. 220 (RH); VIII, p. 75 (C&W).

movement: it gives priority back to form, to metaphysical language, to the instruments of signification over the things signified, to the moralizing evaluation over the knowledge of the true origin. In short, it presents the means as sufficient to itself and the result as freely produced by the illusory image which simply accompanies it.

VI

Sauf . . . ce capitonnage affectif. Mystère des mystères . . . Mais n'est-ce point le meilleur, et le pire, direz-vous?

Except . . . this affective upholstering. Mystery of mysteries . . . But wouldn't you say that it's the best and the worst?

STÉPHANE LUPASCO

Chapter VI

THE TRUTH ABOUT
OTHER PEOPLE

A CCORDING TO PROUST, friendship does not exist. Or, more accurately, it exists but he despises it, regards it as deadly. The company of men for whom he only feels a vague sympathy—and an immense curiosity—is not condemned (and how could it be because without it what would *Remembrance of Things Past* have been made of?), or rather it is condemned simply on account of the loss of time in which it involves us. Friendship, on the other hand, is condemned on more serious grounds: it is harmful because it devours the substance of our most personal and intimate thought. After a three-hour conversation with Saint-Loup, the narrator has an exhausting feeling that he has expended by mere chance, without any goal and without any joy, a little of the strength and the ideas that he was duty bound to hold in reserve for his work. Not that he is lacking in affection for Saint-Loup, or at any rate for his first version of Saint-Loup, or for Charlus, or Swann, or even for Bloch, or again for that friend of Saint-Loup's at Doncières and the long conversation with him which enables the narrator to describe so well the start of his friendship with Saint-Loup: one of those

... *sympathies entre hommes qui, lorsqu'elles n'ont pas d'attrait physique à leur base, sont les seules qui soient tout à fait mystérieuses.*

... intuitive sympathies between man and man which, when they are not based upon physical attraction, are the only kind that is altogether mysterious.[1]

[1] II, p. 104; *The Guermantes Way*: I, p. 788 (RH); V, pp. 135–6 (C&W).

Yet in spite of the undeniable reality of the affection, friend-
ship does not offer us anything essential and is a betrayal of
ourself.

The reason for the contempt, which is expressed with such
frequency in *Remembrance of Things Past*, is really rather puerile.
It is simply that for Proust friendship means practically one
thing only: being a brilliant conversationalist—and in whose
eyes, good heavens!—"exchanging ideas at table" or in some
salon. He feels weary after spending the whole of his evening
developing his ideas on artistic creation for Robert's benefit.
The drama of the *honnête homme* evidently lies in confusing the
pleasure of being together with the business of thinking together
and of eventually providing one another with information,
which is something that could very well happen with two people
who do not feel any friendship for one another. His weariness
stems to a large extent from the perpetual confusion (to which
he is condemned by frequenting the leisure class) between
methodical discussion and gossip. It comes from indulging in
gossip when discussing questions which can only be handled
methodically, and by people whose information is more or less
equal. But if Proust, at the age of forty, has not yet understood
what he should have understood at twenty, if he is still flounder-
ing in this confusion, if he takes the trouble to reply with ideas
when his neighbor at table, or a fellow guest at a private party,
asks him about his views on Sophocles and Leonardo da Vinci,
we can only deplore the persistence of this juvenile naïveté in a
writer who is otherwise so intelligent and mature. There are
good reasons for the narrator's dislike of the idea of discussing
his thought in depth. When one achieves a personal system of
thought, a vision, a sense of life as a whole, one cannot bring
them out in relation to some isolated point because other people
are surprised by them. They fail to understand that you are
referring to a larger view of things and only regard what you
are saying as the adoption of a negative position, a rejection of
what they know; in short, a "paradox." It follows that it is im-
possible to express oneself without communicating simulta-
neously the whole and the details, that is to say, by means of a

work, and one has to make up one's mind only to deal in conversation with unimportant matters. But it does not mean that you would be unwilling or unable to make yourself understood by an interlocutor who was sufficiently interested in what you had to say to him, and with profit to yourself, as Montaigne often insists.

Moreover, Proust never imagines that he has anything at all to learn from another person. He seems to deny that you can learn anything by a method which you have not devised yourself or learnt from books. Yet the conversational method is often more rapid and more lasting than the other two. It is, indeed, probably the only chance we have in life of forging ahead without stopping, by appropriating to ourselves an experience which is not ours. However, if the narrator denies this possibility, he knows about it because he admits that Bloch in literature and Swann in art have enabled him to gain years of time. Now the accelerated transmission of the experience of another person, thanks to which we discover in a matter of days something which for a very long time will provide our mind with nourishment and leave its mark on the whole of our personality (there are definitive habits which can be acquired in a few seconds), is only truly realisable under the high pressure of friendship which alone can ensure that the ideas, by coming together and incorporating themselves into an individual style, become transferable. This speeding up of maturity, of sensibility and intelligence, which is almost always an illusion in love, is not so in friendship.

Unfortunately, Proust comes off badly with Robert, I who is very amiable, affectionate, full of vitality, but intellectually rather limited although, alas, desperately anxious to have "points of view" explained to him. Proust's "fatigue," being of the kind it is, is simply due to the intellectual standard of the people with whom he mixes. It is one of those rare instances when we catch him in the process of using the inconveniences of the leisure life to draw a conclusion about human relationships which he mistakenly believes to be universally valid. His book even bears signs of the bad company he keeps. When he describes

to us for the nth time his theories of art, states all over again,
with the utmost solemnity, that it is very bad not to understand
that writing *Madame Bovary* is not something which can be done
alone, that it is something far more difficult than dazzling one's
listeners at a dinner in town, that it does not call into play in us
the same kind of effort and thought; or again, when he forces
us to listen for the hundredth time, in the greatest detail, to the
theory that original works are not always enjoyed by a large
public at the time of their first appearance, what conclusions
are we to draw if not that Proust is so accustomed to conversing
with imbeciles that he has contracted the disease of endlessly
rehashing the most over-simple of ideas and tirelessly taking up
again the exposition of the crudest of theories by judging it
necessary to embark on interminable explanations. So much the
worse for him and for us, but we are free to deny the validity of
the experience on account of the defective quality of the
Proustian guinea-pigs.

PROUST'S REJECTION OF FRIENDSHIP is based in addition on
more serious grounds, on the conviction that we can never
manage to discover the truth about other people, or other people
the truth about ourselves, and that lying is therefore at the base
of all relations with other people.

To tell the truth, the others are secretive rather than liars. In
any case, they are in no sense incomprehensible. It is not their
character, it is not their feelings, their motives, their passions,
their thoughts which are unknowable; it is the use they make of
their time. Nobody is less of a believer than Proust in the
mystery of the inner man. What human beings feel, want, their
inner states which they think they have concealed, can be read
in their mimicry, their intonations, their facial expressions, and
their verbal habits. Proust is among the most impressionable of
literary witnesses of behavior, or rather it never occurs to him
to separate behavior from feeling. His writing is a demonstra-
tion of the inanity of the theoretical and abstract distinction
between the psychological and the objective novel. Take, for
example, this description of a particular feature of Charlus's:

Je m'aperçus alors que ses yeux, qui n'étaient jamais fixés sur l'inter-
locuteur, se promenaient perpétuellement dans toutes les directions, comme
ceux de certains animaux effrayés, ou ceux de ces marchands en plein air qui,
tandis qu'ils débitent un boniment et exhibent leur marchandise illicite,
scrutent, sans pourtant tourner la tête, les différents points de l'horizon par
où pourrait venir la police.

I noticed then that his eyes, which were never fixed on the person
to whom he was speaking, strayed perpetually in all directions,
like those of certain animals when they are frightened, or those of
street hawkers who, while they are bawling their patter and
displaying their illicit merchandise, keep a sharp look-out, though
without turning their heads, on the different points of the horizon,
from any of which may appear, suddenly, the police.[1]

Proust is describing at the same time the "exterior" and the
"interior," or rather he fortunately does not pose the false
problem of their separation. He does exactly what each of us
would do in similar circumstances: he only interests himself in
the sight of gestures in so far as he has a simultaneous perception
or presentiment of their psychological significance without
which he would not even see what was in front of him, would
not even be aware of it. Once again we observe that the opposi-
tion between the psychological and the behaviorist novel is
purely academic because the more of a psychologist one is, the
more sensitive one is like Proust to behavior, to its details, its
endless diversity. But on the other hand, when he talks about
his feelings, his starting point is his subjective attitude, his
"interiority" (and it is difficult to see how he could have done
otherwise except by a trick of narration), but he relates it as
though it were a succession of events at the same time that he
describes his own actions and what comes to him from out-
side.

There is no pure interiority in Proust and therefore nothing
about the inner secret of people, at any rate not directly.
Against this, there are serious difficulties in informing oneself
about their actions. If I have known some one for a long time,
it becomes more and more easy to share his feelings, but I shall
never be in a position to say on oath what my best friend or my

[1] I, p. 759; *Within a Budding Grove*: I, p. 574 (RH); IV, pp. 79–80 (C&W).

mistress was doing yesterday at five o'clock. In this respect, meetings which are the result of chance or revelations which are equally fortuitous and the result of time, will always have surprises in store for me. When the narrator asks Albertine: "What are you thinking about, darling?" and she replies, "Nothing," it does not mean that human thought is of its nature indescribable—Albertine's thought would be very easy to formulate—but that everybody, even the person who is dearest to us, always hides from us part of what he is doing or plotting. In a word, in Proust there is no psychological mystery about people, but a moral mystery. Our subjective *states* have nothing enigmatic about them, but it is impossible to imagine of what *actions* we are capable.

The truth—the *biographical* truth about those whom we love, which is the only kind that matters—is something that we only discover very partially and very belatedly because at the time when the truth would be of capital importance to us everything, beginning with our own thirst for information, conspires to hide it from us. The essential facts, the things over which doubt has seared our hearts with a red hot iron, are something that for most of the time we shall never know with certainty. Swann will die without knowing whether "on that night" Odette was really sleeping with Forcheville. The oral tradition, which is largely a matter of fantasy, the investigations that passion drives us into undertaking, and more often still scraps of ill-natured gossip occasionally bring us a few fragments of information. For the rest, the reports contradict one another in almost every instance. Supposing it is a question of finding out whether Saint-Loup was already a pederast at the time of *Within a Budding Grove* and whether it was in order to make love with the lift-boy that he shut himself up in the dark-room at Balbec on the pretext of developing photographs? In order to convince myself of the truth or otherwise, the only things I have to go on are the divergent statements of the presumed accomplice and the head waiter. "*Est-ce le liftier ou Aimé qui ment?* (Either the lift-boy had lied, or it was Aimé who was lying)."[1] That is how the problem

[1] III, p. 681; *The Sweet Cheat Gone*: II, p. 859 (RH); IX, p. 362 (C&W).

presents itself to me when I want to find out the truth about my best friend.

It is not surprising therefore that the truth about other people, "*cette vérité que les trois quarts des gens ignorent* (the truth being almost always something that to three people out of four is unknown),"[1] escapes us and all the more frequently because "people" believe in their false ideas about their fellows with a strength which is proportionate to the inaccuracy or even the unlikeliness of their information. It sounds as though we were listening to Pythagoras, according to whom all one is authorized to say about the real is that it is not "even like that," when we find Proust citing, in the guise of a sample of the way in which men work out their beliefs about one another, the news that

> . . . *dans le peuple roumain le nom de Ronsard est connu comme celui d'un grand seigneur tandis que son œuvre poétique y est inconnue. Bien plus, la noblesse de Ronsard repose en Roumanie sur une erreur.*
>
> . . . among the people of Rumania . . . the name of Ronsard is known as that of a great nobleman, while his poetical work is unknown there. Not only that, the Rumanian estimate of Ronsard's nobility is founded upon an error.[2]

This accounts for the disconcerting metamorphoses in *Remembrance of Things Past*: metamorphoses which are as much the result of the confusion of our information as of the personalities. The question is not settled by finding out whether Saint-Loup's amorous practices have really undergone a change or whether he has always been a homosexual and if it is simply that I have come to hear of it belatedly. We get to know people by a succession of characteristics which reach us in fragments linked by huge gaps. No reason, no necessity, no order decide the choice, the frequency, the importance, the number of these revelations. We are therefore perpetually exposed to registering a fact capable of reversing our opinion of people whom we see every day. It is probably in order to make this constant change in the appearance of people look as spectacularly attractive as possible that Proust pushes the suddenness and completeness of

---

[1] III, p. 1023; *Time Regained*: p. 252 (RH); p. 438 (C&W).

[2] II, p. 902; *Cities of the Plain*: II, p. 215 (RH); VIII, p. 67 (C&W).

the changes to the point at which they become unconvincing. And it is their unpredictable, fundamentally unbelievable and unexpected nature that cause the retrospective fears of the narrator when faced with life's "coincidences." It was the very evening when the Princesse de Guermantes tried to kill herself on his account that M. de Charlus was courting a hideous bus conductor in a cab. It is always precisely the famous day when my mistress was so loving, when I believed myself more certain than ever of her love, that she went back to X in a bathing hut. In Proust other peoples' enigmas often descend to the same level as the stratagems of a lower middle-class wife of a head clerk who in addition has two lovers at the same time—the Parisian de Becque.

THE INACCURATE INFORMATION about their fellows generally takes the worst direction: it canonises the bad, places the laurel of genius on the heads of imbeciles, offers "*à la Patrie*" Cottard, "killed at the front," when he has never left the Verdurins' salon, and attributes the partial ruin of the narrator to his ambition to rise above his station, to live on a grand scale in order to dazzle the nobility when in fact he has ruined himself out of love for a girl whose social standing is well below his own. As for the truths that have been checked, established by the narrator, they never fail to blacken the picture of the other person, always show that he is less estimable than one originally thought. Against a revelation which makes certain individuals appear a little less abject than one thought—the streak of generosity in the Verdurins who without anyone knowing provide Saniette with a small income—there are a score of shattering discoveries, and *Remembrance of Things Past* as a whole moves step by step in the direction of an inexorable degradation of the moral standing of its characters.

There are only very few of them who are not three-quarters torn to shreds by the end of the book. Evil pushed to the point of crime, the lack of any sort of honesty in their convictions, the falseness of most of their talents, culture, tastes and ideas add up to a picture of humanity which is all the more discouraging because nobody, not even the historian, will know or will ever be able to establish the truth. In the present, as in the future, vice will always be taken for virtue, genuine talent for borrowed talent, unless there are coincidences which are due to the mutual cancellation of two errors. What excessive simplicity on the part of an author who is considered to be as subtle as Proust (his merit in my opinion consists rather in possessing, in certain cases, a solid good sense and in refusing to accept too seductive interpretations of his work), what naïveté in his manner of accepting the mechanical and inevitable falsification of peoples' biography without ever envisaging for a single moment that our knowledge of this biography might have other sources than the gossip of the salons and tittle-tattle on the beaches.

But whether the truth is known or not, what counts is the author's conception of it. Which are the characters in *Remembrance of Things Past* with whom one would still be prepared to shake hands? First, the saints: the grandmother and the mother who are outside life, who are stars of pure goodness. Next the martyr: Vinteuil who belongs to the ranks of the creators, those whose sordid or vulgar actions, if they are guilty of them, are redeemed by their genius: Bergotte and Elstir. After that come the two principal characters in the book: Swann and Charlus (for Albertine, who is not a bad girl after all and is not stupid, does not leave a very vivid image in the reader's mind or the memory of a particularly rich story). Both have one thing in common: the genuineness of their culture. The times when Swann talks about architecture, when the baron speaks of music, are among the rare conversations about art and literature to which we can listen in *Remembrance of Things Past* without having the feeling that we are listening to poseurs or naïve characters. Swann and Charlus are both really intelligent men —though the baron's intelligence is somewhat damaged by his dementia—because what causes distress with all the others is that they can create an illusion for a certain time, but in the end turn out to be so stupid!

The quality, however, which in Proust's heart, as in Montaigne's, stands for morality, the only one which arouses his deepest sympathy, is goodness—the goodness which in spite of the follies and wrong actions due to wounded pride or spite, transfigures and saves Charlus. In order to complete the list, would we agree to shake hands with Jupien? He is not particularly good, but nevertheless Proust saves him, perhaps because this man of the people expresses himself naturally in a pure and elegant French.

As for the rest, the explanation that Proust gives of them comes down to Rochefoucauld's. Their goodness, especially the *"simple maturation qui finit par sucrer des natures plus primitivement acides que celle de Bloch* (simple maturation which in the end sweetens characters originally more acid even than that of Bloch),"[1] is never anything more than the benevolence caused by the decline of appetites, the satiety of pleasure and money, the soothing of a self-respect which has reached the limit, and fatigue. The honesty of their convictions, their interest in truth, their concern for justice, are always composed of the same stuff as the Dreyfusism of Saint-Loup or Bontemps, which means changing one's political morality as one changes mistresses or jobs. Or again there is the professional conscience of the doctors who give a sigh of relief when they hear that the patient whose death they had prognosticated is indeed dead, and on the other hand are annoyed when somebody whom they thought was buried a year ago in the Père Lachaise raises his hat to them; or finally, the esteem and friendship of the Duchesse de Guermantes for Swann whose approaching death, announced suddenly just before the start of a soirée, did not delay her arrival for a moment.

WHEN WE ASK OURSELVES what motive induces the characters in *Remembrance of Things Past* to meet regularly, since according to Proust friendship is non-existent, what their aim is in meeting, what pleasure they get out of spending hours together, we end by arriving at the only answer which applies to all Proustian gatherings: people come together in order to give themselves up to wickedness. Wickedness is the driving force which is common

[1] III, p. 969; *The Past Recaptured*: p. 209 (RH); p. 364 (C&W).

to so many soirées, at homes, afternoon parties, garden parties, dinners, which all, in spite of the variety of the milieux, the social levels, the number of people taking part, the occasions, whether it is in town or in the country, seem to possess a single aim. It is to produce a sort of caricature of the pleasures which they are supposed to create, to offer a perverted image, the poisoned residue of ancient and forgotten customs. It is in Proust that we find the best and most circumstantial example of the ultimate decadence of fêtes in Western European high society: the total inversion of the very principle of the fête, those anti-fêtes which consist of people coming together in order to devote themselves intensely to the business of wronging one another. Each is preoccupied before all else with securing little triumphs of cruelty and avoiding himself the cruelty of others.

The Proustian fêtes no longer satisfy even the need of display-ing one's material prosperity, the good cheer and luxury that Thorstein Veblen studied about the same period under the title of "conspicuous consumption" in the new-born American high society. One might almost speak of conspicuous destruction of goods because "conspicuous consumption" evokes the *potlatch* ceremony in which those dazzling exhibitions of wastage are rooted. At these fêtes people are bored, but at least they can eat and drink. In Proust we never see anything but a few ghostly *petits fours* being handed round—simple allusions to an age in which humanity was well fed. As for drinks, it is certainly not in order to get drunk that the guests in *Remembrance of Things Past* prolong those soirées from which champagne is brutally absent, having given place to orangeade, strawberry and cherry drinks which are delicious, but not exactly stimulating. A few vague musical pretexts, whatever the narrator's interest in the works performed, are not sufficient either to justify the parties, or rather these mob assemblies, because once the only selection dictated by snobbery has been made, the amphitryons of *Remembrance of Things Past* do not bother themselves in the slightest degree about the conditions governing numbers or relationships which ought to be observed at a gathering of human beings in a civilized society in order to make it agreeable or eventually profitable. No conversations therefore except stupid and futile ones can blossom at these anti-fêtes; the fixed idea of the participants consists for each of them in the pleasure of being present when other people are excluded. Their principal occupation is looking round to see who is there, who has been left out, who has not turned up in spite of being invited —a snub for the masters of the house—whom it is surprising or scandalous to find there, which makes the masters of the house guilty of setting a trap by inviting you with people with whom you cannot associate. In the salons, which enjoy a prominent position in society and to which in principle all those who receive an invitation are only too happy to go, the exultant cruelty is exercised at the expense of those who are left out. Second-class hosts, on the other hand, tremble at the idea of being short of people, and during the Princesse de Guermantes' fête we see Mme de Saint-Euverte recruiting guests for her own garden party which is to take place the following day. In order to gauge the elevated nature of the preoccupations and the refinement of the practices that we expect to find in this domain, it is sufficient to recall that when he receives a card inviting him to this same party at the Princesse de Guermantes', the narrator begins by feeling afraid that it is a trick on the part of somebody who has sent him the card in the hope of seeing him escorted to the door by one of the Guermantes' footmen. Uneasy and anxious to be clear about the position, he seeks out the Duc de Guermantes who hates to compromise himself and refuses by means of various subterfuges and evasions to put the question directly to his brother, the prince, and charitably leaves Marcel in his embarrassing state.

The "revellers" spend their time spying on one another in the hope of enjoying the humiliation of one or other of their number. Their hope is often mistaken for a reality: when the Prince de Guermantes takes Swann aside (in order to talk about the Dreyfus case), the word goes round the salons that it is in order to "throw him out". Even physical accidents are enough to move witnesses to ecstasy. The Grand-duc Wladimir roars with laughter when he catches sight of Mme d'Arpajon with her evening dress completely drenched by a sudden gust of wind blowing on the Hubert Robert fountain. The grand duke then feels that he ought to sympathise with her and shouts: *"Bravo la vieille!"* M. de Charlus comments in a strident tone on the supposed filthiness of a lady who standing close by does not miss a single one of the baron's remarks but, on account of his powerful position in society, she swallows the gratuitous insult without a word. The compliments are as flippant as the scurrilities: the Princesse de Guermantes calls out in the direction of one of the salons: *"'Madame de Villemur! M. Detaille, en grand peintre qu'il est, est en train d'admirer votre cou'* ('Madame de Villemur! M. Detaille, with his wonderful painter's eye, has just been admiring your neck')."[1]

A certain art of party-giving would be a possible aesthetic justification for the society which Proust describes. But this society does not have fun any more than it works, does not enjoy itself any more than it creates. And we cannot avoid recalling by way of contrast that the sense of fêtes was very lively at this period among the working classes as described by Zola, for example, only a little earlier. While Proust's snobs meet in order to cultivate their bad feelings, Zola's workers organise lush repasts which are one of the chief *raisons d'être* of fêtes: forgetting insults, overcoming rancor, exalting material generosity and kindly feeling.

RELATIONSHIPS BETWEEN MEN therefore do not justify themselves by friendship, esteem or pleasure. There is, however, no reason why our behavior should conform to this pessimistic and over-simple conclusion, and when we have barely had time to formulate it we hasten to rejoin those whom we must still describe as friends and whom we cannot do without. Proust needs this pessimism less in order to live than to write. If in fact no truth, no decency, can be expected from relations between human beings, what remains? There is no metaphysical outlet in Proust which converts negative into positive. It is as well to remember it because some interpreters have gone as far as to

[1] II, p. 657; *Cities of the Plain*: II, p. 28 (RH); VII, p. 49 (C&W).

see in Proust a religious writer. In virtue of what I have
described in another place as the argument of Bélise[1]—an argu-
ment according to which it is precisely because somebody is
indifferent to something that he is haunted by it—people have
gone to the length of seeing in Proust a Christian writer.

Now, just as Proust is one of those rare French writers of his
generation who did not succumb to a bellicose chauvinism, he
kept his distance equally from any kind of spiritual tingling
which about 1920 began to irritate the mucous membrane of the
national intelligence and which was shortly going to spray over
French literature lashings of holy water which is still dripping
from it everywhere. Since Proust only wrote definitively about
what he had been able to see for himself—the truly prosaic
element which kills interest in a work being of course not fidelity
to observation, but mythological indiscretion and decorative
affirmation—he has never invoked immortality except in the
vaguest terms, and we might say of them that they are more a
matter of linguistic habit than explicit beliefs. It is difficult to
see anything more than a polished funeral oration in the vaguely
Rousseauist and Kantian passage which follows the account of
Bergotte's death and in the argument, which is romantic at
bottom and very dead and official in form, drawn from the
artist's conscience in favor of a not unlikely survival. We can
see nothing in Proust which goes beyond what the poets of
antiquity wrote when he mentions in fleeting and imprecise
terms *"ces mystères qui n'ont probablement leur explication que dans
d'autres mondes* (those mysteries whose explanation is to be found
probably only in words other than our own)."[2]

In Proust, as in Montaigne, the idea of death is constant, but
as with Montaigne death is a pure fact about which we can say
nothing. The death of other people is hardly distinguishable
from their absence: the loss of a person with whom we are in

---

[1] See *Le Style du Général*, Paris, 1959, p. 69. In Molière's *Les Femmes
savantes*, the old maid, Bélise, says of her lovers, who only exist in her imagina-
tion: "Ils m'ont su révérer si fort jusqu'a ce jour/Qu'ils ne m'ont jamais dit
un mot de leur amour. (They have revered me so deeply up to this very
day/That they have never said a word about their love for me)."

[2] II, p. 1032; *The Past Recaptured*, p. 60 (RH); p. 452 (C&W).

love affects us in the same way as death. The different somer-
saults of suffering up to the final separation and oblivion, the
different stages through which one must pass in order to deserve
indifference, the different thorn bushes and thick woodland that
one has to traverse are the same in both cases. There is no
intrinsic difference between our consciousness of the death of
another person and our consciousness of a final separation from
a living being. As for our own death, the idea of it accompanies
us everywhere; there is no way of avoiding or softening it.
Mythological and philosophical constructions are obviously
capers to relieve our anxiety in face of the intolerable. It is a
sign of slight progress if we are able to stay fairly quiet. Proust
treats it in much the same way as passion. He does not evade the
problem any more than he imagines that he has the right to
solve it according to his fancy, once he consents to take notice
of it (which is what characterizes the philosophical mind). Like
passion, death is a question of fact and not of principle. The
constant dissolution of the ego, that is to say, of affectivity in
the sense of loss of interest in the emotions unceasingly reducing
the past to indifference—for *"ce sont les paradis perdus où l'on se
sentirait perdu* (they are the lost paradises where one would feel
oneself lost)"—provides us perhaps with an experience which is
analogous to death.[1] At the same time, this experience helps us
a little to support the idea of our annihilation because it proves
to us that indifference to life could precede it and render its loss
bearable, and that perhaps the imminence even of death, pre-
ceded a short time before by the breaking of our links with our
own emotions, *"nous guérira du désir de l'immortalité* (will cure us
of the desire for immortality)."[2] In addition, Proust makes us
understand in this way that, subjectively, not all deaths are the
same or are all suffered in the same mood; that popular wisdom
is not perhaps wrong in distinguishing between the death of a
young person and that of an old man, between an accidental
and a natural death, the death which strikes and that for which
one prepares oneself, however feeble the nature of the prepara-

[1] II, p. 859; *Cities of the Plain*: II, p. 186 (RH); VIII, p. 8 (C&W).
[2] III, p. 645; *The Sweet Cheat Gone*: II, p. 835 (RH); XI, p. 316 (C&W)

tion, which is an invitation to distinguish between them by taking into account the organic suffering, which is probably very great, that comes from the mere fact of dying.

The inevitable change in the ego attaches itself or leads to the impossibility of getting to know the truth about other people, for the simple reason that I myself am the first among the other people. There is nothing in these psychological considerations which is not thoroughly banal. The difficulty lies in giving meaning to life while taking account of these facts. We know that for Proust personally the means of achieving it, of making life interesting at the same time that one makes death indifferent, was to produce a work of art.

To be sure, we never accustom ourselves to the idea of death. Even when the narrator can say "*l'idée de la mort s'installa définitivement en moi* (the idea of death took up permanent residence in me)," he adds, "*non que j'aimasse la mort, je la détestais* (not that I loved death, I abhorred it)."[1] Nor is it in the manner of the poets of antiquity and the Renaissance that he rejoices in the idea that posterity will perpetuate his memory: the judgement of posterity on his work is as indifferent to him— from that point of view—as the judgement of his contemporaries. It is by a misuse of words that one seeks to persuade oneself that artistic creation cures the fear of dying. Inversely, the sense of approaching death engenders in the narrator dispositions which permit him to devote himself assiduously to his work.

[1] III, p. 1042; *The Past Recaptured*: p. 267 (RH); p. 465 (C&W).

VII

Un homme né sensible et qui n'aurait pas d'imagination pourrait malgré celà écrire des romans admirables.
A man who is born sensitive and without imagination could in spite of all that write admirable novels.
PROUST, The Past Recaptured

. . . L'affaiblissement de la sensibilité, qui est la banqueroute du talent.
. . . The weakening of sensibility which is the bankruptcy of talent.
PROUST, Contre Sainte-Beuve

Chapter VII

THE WORK OF ART

PROUST continually asserts—it is one of the ideas to which he clings most strongly—that the work of art comes from a "deeper self" which is different from the everyday self, is a stranger to ordinary conversation, and without any connection with the personality that we habitually display to other people. The drawing of this hermetic frontier between the two selves which are so distinct from one another that to allow either of them (say, the creative self) to speak, would mean silencing the other. Conversely, the absolute separation of the deeper from the superficial everyday self would probably be more convincing if we did not observe on every page of *Remembrance of Things Past* that it is from the everyday self that the deeper self obtains its most lucid information. We find ourselves wondering what Proust's creative self would do if the everyday self were not there to provide it with information. For it is not from "the secret country," innocent of all contact with experience, that the Proustian creative self, I imagine, drew Cottard's puns, Baron de Charlus's gait, Mme Verdurin's laugh, M. de Norpois's eloquence, the "bricks" of the manager of the Grand Hotel, and the description of the Guermantes' salon. Everything takes place as though Proust, while paying tribute to one aesthetic, practised another which was the opposite of it. He appears, in *Swann's Way*, to start from a Nervalian conception of his work: a lyrical, visionary, melodious conception that invests things with an emotional and discreetly unreal halo. But as the work progresses, it is more and more the realistic and precise memoir-writer whose voice we hear; more and more Saint-Simon who carries the day in Proust and ousts Nerval. As early as "A Love

Affair of Swann's" we feel that he is more at his ease in the
portrayal of "the little cell" than in the heavy handed attempts
to use the names of Norman towns in order to produce evocative
poetry. Passages such as the description of the waters of the
Vivonne, to which the narrator clings most firmly and seems to
regard as the heart of his work, might have been signed by
Henri de Régnier or a pupil of Régnier's. What reader of
Proust does not wilt today when, on turning a page, he catches
sight of the outline of the crushing and uncrushable hawthorn
bushes which is like the menacing silhouette of a merciless bore
emerging at a street corner?

Curiously enough, Proust's style, which is full of felicitous
turns of phrase and without the least effort places in front of our
eyes everything that the author wants us to see when it is a
question of describing people, suddenly becomes heavy, blind
and breathless the moment that it is used to describe an object
or nature. Thus in the middle of the account of the soirée at the
Princesse de Guermantes, when the parade of guests, gestures
and words is so lively, so patently right that we even forget
about the style because we are reaping the benefits of it without
feeling the need to ask questions about its value, Proust suddenly
embarks on the description of the Hubert Robert fountain.
Something seems to snap; the writer's tone changes; he has
made up his mind to produce what he considers a "purple
passage". And that in fact is precisely what he does:

> *Dans une clairière réservée par de beaux arbres dont plusieurs étaient aussi
> anciens que lui, planté à l'écart, on le voyait de loin, svelte, immobile,
> durci, ne laissant agiter par la brise que la retombée plus légère de son
> panache pâle et frémissant.*

> In a clearing surrounded by fine trees several of which were as
> old as itself, set in a place apart, one could see it in the distance,
> slender, immobile, stiffened, allowing the breeze to stir only the
> lighter fall of its pale and quivering plume.[1]

This inevitably recalls Jean Nesmy, Maurice Bouchor or Ernest
Pérochon, those underground writers whose names only survive
in the French schoolbooks of the very young because they are at

[1] II, p. 656; *Cities of the Plain*: II, p. 43 (RH); VII, p. 78 (C&W).

once inoffensive, full of descriptions which are eminently suitable for cutting up into tiny fragments that can be used for dictation. As for the rest of the description of the Hubert Robert fountain, all we can say is that it is practically unintelligible, not because of its excessive subtlety, but because of the writer's inability to produce a coherent picture from all the ponderous comparisons in which he submerges himself. We are obliged, in fact, to treat the phrases like the pieces of a puzzle in order to extract any sort of visual impression from them at all. Worst of all, the natural style seems suddenly to desert the author in the course of the passage which fortunately is not overlong.

Proust wrote, "*Je crois que la métaphore seule peut donner une sorte d'éternité au style* (I think that metaphor alone can give style a sort of eternity)."[1] But if *Remembrance of Things Past* really depended on metaphor to give it a sort of eternity, the eternity would amount to very much of a compromise. If we drew up a list of Proustian metaphors, we should be astounded by the gaffs and the lack of taste that he betrays when he uses imagery, or simply the abundance of platitudes in which he indulges when, for example, he speaks of "*cette brillante étoile qui, à l'instant du réveil, éclaire derrière le dormeur son sommeil tout entier* (that bright star which at the moment of waking illuminates behind the sleeper),"[2] or "*quand, par les soirs d'été, le ciel harmonieux gronde comme une bête fauve* (when, on a summer evening, the resounding sky growls like a tawny lion),"[3] or again when he compliments the sea "*sur les sommets neigeux de ses vagues en pierre d'émeraudes* (upon the snowy crests of its emerald waves),"[4] or finally when he gives way to a bewildering flight of imagination in this manner:

Symbole soit de cette invasion que prédisait le défaitisme de M. de Charlus, soit de la coopération de nos frères musulmans avec les armées de la France, la lune étroite et recourbée comme un sequin semblait mettre le ciel parisien sous le signe oriental du croissant.

[1] "A propos du Style de Flaubert" in *Chroniques*, p. 193.
[2] II, p. 336; *The Guermantes Way*: I, p. 957 (RH); VI, p. 34 (C&W).
[3] I, p. 186; *Swanns Way*: I, p. 142 (RH); I, p. 255 (C&W).
[4] I, p. 672; *Within a Budding Grove*: I, p. 510 (RH); III, p. 351 (C&W).

Symbol perhaps of the invasion foretold by the defeatism of M. de
Charlus, or else of the co-operation of our Mussulman brothers
with the armies of France—the moon, narrow and curved like a
sequin, seemed to have placed the sky of Paris beneath the oriental
sign of the crescent.[1]

Whatever his own views, it is not when he is being metaphorical
that Proust is a great writer; it is not when he is being poetical
that he is original and has something to teach us; it is when he is
being realistic, when he is the narrator and chronicler that he is
the great writer.

IT IS BECAUSE the author of *Remembrance of Things Past* had
shown his commentators the way too clearly that they have tried
passionately to discover in his book all the things which are not
there or, if they are, are not the true source of its originality.
Nothing is more instructive in this respect than comparisons
between Proust and other writers. He has been compared to
Henry James, possibly because they are both considered to be
"complicated." Instead, however, of criticizing him for a
decadent Byzantinism, it would be more to the point to criticize
Proust for a tendency to caricatural simplicity, for the naïveté
of his themes, and more often than the abuse of allusiveness for
an excessively repetitive explanation of his personal views.

He has also been compared to Joyce. Now it must be said
firmly that in spite of the torrent of rhetoric released by the
famous and mythical "rose-window composition"—a modest
way of suggesting that it is a collection of bits and pieces of
doubtful color and several flights of fancy freely pursued to the
limit—questions of form and structure play no part at all in
Remembrance of Things Past. In any case, what literary work of
lasting interest has ever been the product of exclusively formal
preoccupations? When we speak of form in the novel or in
poetry, we are inclined to overlook the fact that literature is
neither music, painting nor architecture, that words and
sentences are not forms, or are only so in a minor sense, because
they are primarily and essentially conventional signs intended to

[1] III, p. 809; *The Past Recaptured*: p. 86 (RH); p. 147 (C&W).

express ideas and owe their value first and foremost to the value of the ideas expressed. We can only speak of form in literature by analogy. If originality of content is often accompanied by innovations of form, there is no literary revolution which is not in the first place a revolution in content or, to put it baldly, the discovery of an original subject and something new to say. It would not be difficult to show that even in *Ulysses*, where changes in the traditional form of narration are obvious (although the technique of some of the best chapters like the first is similar to Flaubert's and a good many of the others are simply pastiches of different styles: newspaper style, medieval epic style, etc.) it is the novelty of the material and the boldness of thought which at bottom are responsible for the greatness and the revolutionary character of the novel. Nevertheless, the highly distinctive structure of *Ulysses* and the use of the a-syntactic language of the inner monologue make it a book which belongs to an entirely different family from *Remembrance of Things Past*.

When Robert Musil's *The Man without Qualities* was translated into French, the inevitable comparison with *Remembrance of Things Past* did not fail to impress a number of clever people, perhaps because both books contain long sentences. *The Man without Qualities*, however, unfolds in the ambiguous region of symbolism, tries to be, at one and the same time, comical and allegorical—a preoccupation to which Proust was a complete stranger. What Musil is seeking, by means of his description of an historic mileu, are prototypes of attitudes which though social are above all moral and spiritual: Diotima, Clarissa, Arnheim. Unlike Musil, Proust does not go in for prototypes or symbolical figures. In his novel a character is always a particular person. M. de Norpois or Mme Verdurin are types belonging to a period and a society only because they are the people that they are. Proust treats them as individuals. In Musil we do not even find the rich, farcical, buffoon-like comedy which is something that is common to Proust and Joyce (a talent which goes largely unnoticed in both cases) because the comic element in Musil does not possess the giantism of Proustian or Joycean comedy; it is all filigree and arouses silent jubilation much more often than a roar of laughter. When Valery Larbaud and Benjamin Crémieux introduced Italo Svevo to the European reading public, several critics compared him to Proust because in *The Confessions of Zeno* we find ourselves listening to the voice of a man who is trying to reconstruct his past for the benefit of his psychoanalyst. In spite of the enormous differences of tone, style, construction and, most important of all, subject, and though Zeno's past, at the cost of considerable effort, is constantly in the process of being re-discovered *as the past* through the anguish of the awakened dreamer or the blinding flash of some obsessive recollection—while in Proust we are always living in the present—they are brought together simply and solely on account of the fact that they both use the word "memory."

"For us," wrote an Italian critic in 1926, "the term 'analyst' does not have the same meaning or the same importance that it may have in France where criticism had to invent it in order to give status (*sistemare*) to Marcel Proust and his imitators. For us, Manzoni is also an analyst, and one might say that the Italian novel from the *Promessi sposi* to *Lemmonio Boreo* is an analytical novel."

We observe once again the automatism in the bursting out of the words "analytical novel" the moment one is dealing with a writer who is reflective or meditative. Moreover, judging from what he wrote a year later, this critic takes a poor view of the genre: "Italo Svevo, the author of some very mediocre novels . . . is proclaimed a great writer by the execrable Irish poet, Joyce, and an execrable Parisian poet, Valery Larbaud . . . What is Svevo's merit? To have come closer than any other Italian to that passively analytical literature which reached its highest point in Proust."[1]

All these unjustified comparisons, which are based on the identification of works in the name of the most superficial of resemblances, show the persistence of erroneous slogans even in relation to one of the most widely read and most widely discussed of writers. Recently Proust's name came up again in discussions

[1] Guido Piovene, quoted by Bruno Maier in his *Historical Introduction to the Complete Works of Svevo* (Italo Svevo, *Opere*, dall'Oglio editore, Milan).

of the Prince of Lampedusa's pleasantly artificial novel, *The Leopard,* merely because it happened to be a story about the aristocracy.

PROUST ESTABLISHED his distinction between the everyday and the "creative" self in discussing "Sainte-Beuve's Method": the practice of explaining literary works by means of the writers' biographies. But we must distinguish between the particular case of Sainte-Beuve and the general thesis that Proust tries to maintain in refuting Sainte-Beuve.

When treated as a particular example of criticism, *Contre Sainte-Beuve* cannot be faulted. At the time of its posthumous publication in 1954, the book, which is one of the very rare works of criticism produced by our century, with its pages on Nerval and Balzac, met with a cold and pained reception because it demolished the principle underlying a certain kind of French literary history. Although *Contre Sainte-Beuve* was the belatedly discovered work of a classic author, it was treated like the work of a beginner. It was attacked and passed over in silence at one and the same time. I mean by this that it was mentioned with reprobation while care was taken not to say precisely what was in it and for a stronger reason still—the best reason in the world —not to reply to it. We should be on our guard against people who say: "I don't like polemic." It means that they generally prefer a form of insidious equivocation. In reality, people are hostile to polemic because they are short of arguments. Those delicate creatures are content to replace their own non-existent ideas by malicious insinuations and unproven assertions. In addition, "polemic" is not a category of thought; it is a denomination which is external to it and is completely subordinated to the public and the moment. The same page can be read as a list of observations which are sensible but flat, or can be felt as a powerful act of aggression according to the milieu and the period in which it falls. It depends on the degree to which the milieu and the period are impregnated by prejudices and interests which are indirectly threatened. It is above all from the reader that the polemical reverberations come. As for the book itself, what counts is to know whether it does or does not contain arguments and what those arguments are worth. But perhaps we should assume that to take cognizance of an argument or even of a fact is repugnant to some minds which react with the same bad faith to objections described as *"nuancées"* as to objections introduced without any beating about the bush.

The disarray and the consternation provoked by the publication of *Contre Sainte-Beuve* were very quickly overcome. One saw signs here and there, even in articles about completely different subjects, a word or two asserting by way of precaution that the reputation of the author of the *Lundis* was in no way diminished by Proust's work. In an article in one of the best of the French daily papers discussing the problem of finding out whether Sainte-Beuve did or did not eat meat on Good Friday, 10th April, 1868, the author slipped in this comment by way of parenthesis: "[Sainte-Beuve] still holds the top place as a critic. Let us leave on one side Proust's debatable *Contre Sainte-Beuve* which appeared last year."[1] But if the work is debatable why not debate it! Why not prove that Sainte-Beuve was not mistaken about Baudelaire or Balzac or Stendhal or Flaubert! Nothing is easier to define than the conditions which would have to be satisfied by the answer in order to convince us. It would be sufficient, in fact, to demonstrate by examples the opposite of what Proust says in the following passage:

> If all the nineteenth-century literature bar *Les Lundis* had been destroyed by fire, so that it was from the *Lundis* that we had to assess the relative importance of nineteenth-century writers, we should see Stendhal ranked below Charles de Bernard, below Vinet, below Molé, below Mme de Verdelin, below Ramond, Sénac de Meilhan, Vicq d'Azyr, below how many more, and, to tell the truth, none too distinguishable between Alton Shée and Jacquemond.[2]

There always exists in French literature some great and influential critic who functions like some sort of automatic machine and is admirably regulated by his negative reactions to

[1] M. Paul Guilly, *Le Monde*, 8th April, 1955.
[2] *By Way of Sainte-Beuve*, p. 78.

talent. Between the Wars the part was played to perfection by Thibaudet who found a way of avoiding even a mention of Proust in an article published on June 1st, 1919, in which he drew up a balance sheet of the most important French novels published during the 1914–18 war. A balance sheet from which emerged after a very severe sorting-out the three following masterpieces: *Le Justicier* by Paul Bourget, *Solitudes* by Edouard Estaunié and *Fumées dans la campagne* by Edmond Jaloux.[1]

It is a strange thing that the only official critic whom posterity gladly condemns is one of those very rare critics who made no mistakes about his contemporaries: Boileau. If we take any one of his satires, transpose it into our own age, play at replacing seventeenth-century names by their equivalents, it is easy to see that today Boileau would have just as much chance of being turned down by a right wing as by a left wing newspaper. Take this, for example:

> *Bienheureux Scudéri, dont la fertile plume*
> *Peut tous les mois sans peine enfanter un volume!*
> *Tes écrits, il est vrai, sans art et languissants,*
> *Semblent être formés en dépit du bon sens;*
> *Mais ils trouvent pourtant, quoi qu'on en puisse dire,*
> *Un marchand pour les vendre et des sots pour les lire.*
>
> Blessed Scudéri whose fertile pen
> Can give birth to a book every month without pain!
> Your writings, it is true, languid and without art,
> Seem to be formed in spite of good sense;
> But whatever one can say of them, they find
> A merchant to sell and fools to read them.

At the time when these lines were written, Scudéri was the great and fashionable novelist and Boileau, who was twenty-six, was still only the author of three satires whose total length was equal to twenty typewritten pages. Let us translate into twentieth-century idiom this greenhorn's apostrophe:

Dear Monsieur G, or dear Monsieur M. of the French Academy

---

[1] The conclusion is worth quoting: "It would be impossible to imagine anything more different than M. Bourget's laborious and masterly concentration, the methodical, sharp and pitiless penetration of M. Estaunié, the careful, spacious, full and well-balanced narration of M. Jaloux."

(unlike Boileau, I obviously cannot mention names because I am writing in the twentieth century), dear Monsieur A or B, the inexhaustible fecundity of your blacks enables you to publish four books and six hundred articles a year. Of course, nobody thinks of regarding the anaemic ideas and the tepid prose which you sign as anything but the product of a wholesale grocery. Everyone is agreed on this point, and yet you always manage to find a publisher who will get you printed, newspapers which ask you for copy, and imbeciles who buy your stuff.

What bad taste, people would say! It is some envious wretch who is writing insults instead of criticism! And we know that nowadays criticism must remain "constructive," that is to say, must end up with a eulogy. Boileau's frankness when attacking Scudéri is exceeded by the courage he displays in speaking of the all-powerful Chapelain:

> Chapelain veut rimer, et c'est là sa folie.
> Mais, bien que ses durs vers, d'épithètes enflés
> Soient des moindres grimauds chez Ménage sifflés,
> Lui-même il s'applaudit, et, d'un esprit tranquille,
> Prend le pas, au Parnasse, au-dessus de Virgile.
> Chapelain wants to rhyme, and that's his folly.
> But though his harsh verse, bloated with epithets,
> Is hissed at Ménage's by the least of scribblers,
> He applauds himself and with a calm mind
> Takes precedence over Virgil on Parnassus.

It is monstrous plain-speaking. For about 1660 Chapelain not only represented a sort of national literary taboo, as untouchable as Claudel is today: he also exercised considerable temporal power because he held the official job of drawing up the list of writers worthy to receive a pension from the king. He was in a way and at the same time Claudel and M. André Malraux.[1]

Boileau is very different from the person who is described to us as the pompous promulgator of classical dogmas. His independence and intransigence make him the Paul Léautaud of the seventeeth century. But Léautaud always lived apart from the world. He did not reach the general public until 1951 when,

[1] Or better still, M. André Malraux himself. At the time when these lines were written, André Malraux was Minister of Culture.

at the age of eighty, he gave the famous radio interviews whose vivacity and verve cut straight across the post-war critical style. Boileau, on the other hand, became a recognized authority from 1670 onwards. But he did not owe his success to a lukewarm nature or to compromise. We are bound to admit that in the matter of satire and literary criticism the seventeenth century enjoyed more freedom than our own. In the twentieth century a Léautaud is at once classed as a grouser whose amusing reactions are of no importance. That is one of the subtlest forms of censorship and it would be inconceivable today that the author of a work introducing real persons as pitiless as *Les Caractères* would continue to enjoy close relations with and the confidence of the powerful.

Boileau assumed responsibility as a critic and ran the risks that it involved. It was the young writers, the school of beginners whom he began by praising, and made no secret of the fact that he preferred them to everyone who in his view was insignificant.[1] In his writings we never come across any of those timid precautions, those nobly equivocal formulas, described as "*nuancées*," in which bad critics betray a crippling fear of being mistaken, their meager confidence in their own judgement, their defensive reticences which keep in line with the fashionable verdicts or anticipate an evening meeting which might make them change their minds; lastly, their determination always to hold in reserve, in cases of praise or blame, some compensatory corrective in the event of a change of view which is always a possibility.

IF WE LEAVE ON ONE SIDE Sainte-Beuve's particular errors of judgement and go on to examine his general thesis, the principle on which he bases his historical explanation of literary works, we find ourselves hesitating over which of the two, Sainte-Beuve or Proust, gives the more simplified, the more summary and less satisfying view of creative work.

---

[1] In the case of Racine, however, as R. Picard has shown in *La Carrière de Jean Racine*, Boileau's support came rather late. But what strikes us in Boileau is the absolutely forthright and unequivocal way in which he condemns bad writers.

Proust repeats interminably that we cannot identify the every-day and the creative self. Then, when it comes to giving a precise definition of what he means by the everyday self, we observe that according to him it is merely the self which chatters with Mme Cambremer or exchanges a few platitudes with Oriane. But why reduce life in this arbitrary fashion to gossip in hotel lounges and philosophical discussions on café terraces? Proust is amazed when he finds that the "everyday" Bergotte is not the Bergotte of his books. He solemnly meditates on the point, but what he calls "everyday life" is lunch at Odette Swann's! In other words, he accepts the very definition of life given by Sainte-Beuve: life means life in the salon. We are naturally not prevented from asking ourselves why life should not also be walks along the bank of the Vivonne, conversations with Swann, passion, the attraction of women, the sight of the sun shining on the sea, reading Tolstoy, bursts of uncontrollable laughter in front of Norpois and—why not?—literary work. Proust's theory of literary creation is just as summary as his critique of intelligence. If we are willing to accept the definition quietly, that to be intelligent is to understand, it is difficult to see how one could understand, and above all understand other men, without what is called sensibility, intuition, emotions, sensations. If we decide to confine acceptance of the term intelligence to operations described by means of formal logic, it is evident that we did not have to await the arrival of Proust in order to see that Diafoirus was not intelligent. What is more, we know to what reactionary trends the thesis accepted by Proust, as though it were gospel truth, is linked.

Musil, who is much more clearsighted than Proust on this point, satirically places the enunciation of the theories into the mouth of one of his drawing-room idealists:

"You mean," asked Diotima, "that all things considered, the Lord is the equivalent, or almost, of the poem?"
"That's a marvellous word of yours!" replied her friend.[1]
"It's the mystery of the strong life. Intelligence alone is not enough: the essential takes place beyond it. Men who have

[1] Arnheim.

achieved greatness have always loved music, poetry, form, discipline, religion and chivalry."

The Proustian explanation of artistic creation (which in any case is not his own invention) would assume, in order to be coherent, a Platonic brand of metaphysics. The odd thing is that the vast majority of twentieth-century critics take this postulate as their starting point without daring to formulate the metaphysical implications which are indemonstrable and would not stand up to even a summary examination. Whence the language which is confused, imperious, allusive, turgid, peremptory and flabby of an entire system of criticism and which performs at the same time the role of the mysterious and the great-hearted. It is the language of people whose tone of voice is all the more assertive because they do not know what they are asserting. After getting a footing in phenomenology, which has provided it with a rich supply of words, their style has also invaded art criticism. The result is that we speak more rarely than ever of a work, whether book or picture; we use it as a screen on to which we project a verbal film that is more or less identical in every case. It becomes a parasitic and narcissistic criticism which operates at the expense of the work on which one is supposed to be commenting. It feeds on a pseudo-mystery and is induced to give a privileged place to grandiloquent works that provide it with plenty of hay to munch without which it would perish.

This attitude leads Proust himself to put Maeterlinck above Mérimée because Mérimée is too "arid" a spirit while Maeterlinck's prose has a spiritual air. What this means is putting a writer with a moderate talent below an unreadably bogus poet. Another example is provided by Balzac, a writer of whom Proust's opinion varied considerably and whose merits, we might say, are largely the invention of visionary commentators and a criticism which might for once be described as constructive. When we find Proust and M. de Charlus admiring *Les Illusions perdues* or *Les Secrets de la princesse de Cadignan*, our reaction is the same as Saint-Loup's in front of the photo of Albertine:

Il ne fit aucune observation, il avait pris l'air raisonnable, prudent,

*forcément un peu dédaigneux qu'on a devant un malade—eût-il été jusque-là
un homme remarquable et votre ami—mais qui n'est plus rien de tout cela,
car, frappé de folie furieuse, il vous parle d'un être céleste qui lui est apparu
et continue à le voir à l'endroit où vous, homme sain, vous n'apercevez qu'un
édredon.*

He made no remark upon it, he had assumed the reasonable,
prudent, inevitably somewhat disdainful air which we assume
before a sick person—even if he has been in the past a man of
outstanding gifts, and our friend—who is now nothing of the sort,
for, raving mad, he speaks to us of a celestial being who has
appeared to him, and continues to behold this being where we,
the sane man, can see nothing but a quilt on the bed.[1]

When Proust declares that creation is superior to observation,
he makes us understand that by observation he probably means
something rather flat and rudimentary. He only disposes of the
caricature of the novelist-spy prowling round the salons and
"engraving in his memory" profiles and propositions. Moreover,
this is the way in which literary historians often describe the
working out of a book: Molière or Flaubert taking up their
positions at street corners "in order to observe," as one goes to
the Bibliothèque Nationale in order to make notes and put the
substance of an historical work into index forms. It is not the way
in which the author of an original work collects his material
because it is naturally not enough to observe in order to see, and
one often sees much better when one had no intention of
observing. But Proust does not bother to explain to us how he
envisages a process of creation which is entirely unencumbered
by observation. To note that every original artist has his own
themes, his own accent, "the air of the song," which the author
of *Contre Sainte-Beuve* detects "behind the words," simply means
noting that affectivity is the sole form of power, if not the sole
material of artistic creation. The problem is not resolved by
knowing what part of the composition of works of art originates
internally, what part is made up of information (in the widest
sense of the term) which comes from outside, what part again
belonging to what Proust calls the internal production consists
of the crystallization of past emotions and experiences which

[1] III, 437; *The Sweet Cheat Gone*: II, p. 689 (RH); XI, p. 28 (C&W).

were equally external in origin. In any case, the problem is a sterile one when discussed in the abstract because the original dosages of inner and outer differ according to the arts and artists.

The aesthetic vicious circle consists in appealing to the arbitrary or equivocal idea of a "work of art" in general. What connection is there between *Pantagruel* and a Persian carpet? Yet the aesthetician by using both of them will work out the same proposition about "artistic creation," "the experience of the work," the "contact with the work." It seems reasonable to think that the information which comes from outside is of more importance in those art-forms like the novel, which cannot exist without some sort of empirical content, than in art-forms such as the plastic arts and music which depend on structure, form, rhythms, and not primarily on ideas or narrative—that it needs more anecdotal information about human nature to write *Nana* than to compose a sonata.

Now it was precisely the way in which Zola was and still is underestimated that is the result of criticism's contempt for every novelist in whom one seems to detect a predominance of "observation"; contempt whose counterpart is permanent overestimation of writers who are regarded as possessing their own particular "vision". The fact that nowadays the palest, the most anaemic of the novels forming part of a series like the flattest, the most labored and most pedestrian of narratives are regularly hailed as bringing a "new vision," a universe which is completely "new," is significant because it shows in what direction the automatisms of the pen are moving and what vocabulary is utilized for preference by the eulogistic parrotry. The snobbery which wants only the pretended visionaries to be regarded as "blue blooded" has led to limitless complacency with regard to Balzac and a failure to recognize Zola's outstanding qualities— in many cases the very qualities which are gratuitously attributed to Balzac who does not possess them. We can at least come to grips with Zola with our feet on the ground and decide for ourselves on the merit of his books without, as with Balzac, having had our reflexes conditioned in advance by a veritable literature which asserts that it is precisely when the work is stupid that we must find it sublime, and that an unfavorable reaction is nothing but a sign of our own aridity and poverty of imagination.

By declaring that though wishing to be a realist Balzac is in fact a visionary, Baudelaire means that Balzac's vision lends reality a degree of intensity which is too persistent not to be in many cases imaginary, and that in *La Comédie humaine* "each of the characters, even the porters, possesses genius." People have used this phrase of Baudelaire's in order to deify Balzac, as though it were sufficient for an author to project myths, whatever their quality, into reality in order to become unassailable. On the other hand, no one has ever claimed that Zola is a "visionary" for the simple reason that in addition to everything else his vision turns out to be accurate. When he describes for us a crash on the Stock Exchange in *L'Argent*, he is as exalting and manages the *suspense* with as much verve as Balzac: the only difference is that his Stock Exchange crash is true, that a stockbroker would find nothing to alter in his description of the atmosphere and the technical elements of his story; in short, that we can believe what he says whereas in nine times out of ten we cannot believe Balzac who seems to be trying first and foremost to dazzle himself by his story. Also, the famous accelerated observation, with which Balzac is usually credited in order to explain how he has been able to acquire so great a knowledge of the most diverse milieux after studying them so little, belongs to Zola rather than to him. In fact, in the case of Balzac, where is the merit in acquiring in accelerated fashion knowledge which is fifty per cent wrong and expressed with such crude psychology? Zola's knowledge is accurate and forms an unbelievably voluminous mass of material which is surprising in the case of a man who lived a hardworking and orderly life. Zola was still young when he wrote *Nana*, in which we might think that we were sharing the condensed experience of an old buck who had spent sixty years in the little theaters and variety halls.

Nor does anybody willingly emphasize Zola's humor and his comic power: it is supposed to be understood that he is a clod— or Proust's comic power, for that matter, which would diminish his reputation as the poet of the inner life. Now the comic is just as mysterious as poetry. Cottard's play on words, the "bloomers" of the manager of the Grand Hotel are not superior to a good bit of fantasy in a number by Bobino; elementary and refined comedy are made up of the same elements. What farce is coarser than the unfortunate Morel's series of misadventures, dragged hither and thither by all the richest pederasts crowding in on him in *Cities of the Plain*, from the incidents in the brothel to the fictitious duel of M. de Charlus? We know that the enormity of the caricature can end either in vulgarity or the sublime.

WE MUST CONSOLE OURSELVES for finding that Proust took Henri de Régnier, Pierre Loti, and Francis Jammes for very great geniuses by observing that, on the contrary, he is the only great writer who possessed a genuine feeling for painting and the plastic arts in general. Earlier on I deplored Proust's habit—he was copying Ruskin's worst faults—of making social rapprochements between this or that individual in a famous painting and a real person. But this should not blind us to the fact that in general, and apart from his doubtful embroidering of the Giotto frescoes at Padua, his references to pictures are usually of the happiest, the least forced, and reveal at once a sureness of eye, a feeling for the spatial arts, a culture formed by contact with works which is decidedly rare in French literature. Proust excels at giving the equivalent in prose of a picture and he does it with a precision, which is at once evocative and descriptive, that one occasionally finds during the nineteenth century—the golden age of art criticism—in Taine, Fromentin and the Goncourts. I do not know who provided him with the model for Elstir. Blanche claims, mischievously, that it was only Helleu, but in the preface to the book by this same Blanche called *De Dante à Degas*, which is remarkable anyway, Proust mentions "*le grand, l'admirable Picasso*", which shows the originality of his taste, whereas Balzac was only impressed by the price of works of art and Stendhal, who is accepted today as a connoisseur, confined himself to reflecting the taste which was fashionable in his own time.

PROUST'S THEORY OF LITERARY CREATION is an exact re-
versal of Sainte-Beuve's and is on the same level. In reply to the
theory that the work is produced by a self which goes out to
dinners in town, Proust asserts that it is produced by a self which
never eats. But he would have met with much greater difficulties
in discussing the problem with Taine, who is truly a great his-
torian of art and literature, while Sainte-Beuve's error, and
following in its wake the whole of academic literary history, is
not in the least the result of a desire to provide an historical
explanation of the works; their aim in fact is really not to
provide it, not even to tackle it, but to describe an anecdotal
history of the writers as a history of literature. In all histories of
literature people still give cries of joy the day when they estab-
lish, with the documents in their hands, that a poet wrote a sad
poem an hour after receiving his income tax demand.

Remembrance of Things Past itself has not escaped the clouds of
grasshoppers who have been having a good time measuring the
breadth of the walks at Illiers and the height of the waves at
Cabourg. Alas! What makes going for a sail in a boat beautiful
in Maupassant is not sailing in a boat, which is a thing that any-
one can do; it is Maupassant—in spite of the fact that without
the boat Maupassant's story would not have been written. It is
a disturbing paradox that in spite of learned works and whole
libraries of doctoral theses, every time that we want to document
ourselves about an author, it is difficult to find a book which
discusses his work. The majority of those that we come across
seem determined to give a minute account of every aspect of a
writer except the one which makes us want to read a book by
him. The work appears for the most incomprehensible of motives
to be a super-addition from outside on to the life of some
M. X.

In the negative aspect of his criticism of Sainte-Beuve, Proust
is therefore right because there is only one way of talking about
an author and one fundamental condition which must be ful-
filled: what is important to him must be important to you. Talk-
ing about an author means using him as a support for saying
what we ourselves think about the things of which he has spoken.

ABOUT THE AUTHOR

JEAN-FRANÇOIS REVEL is the most prominent young French-
man in the tradition of Jean-Paul Sartre, Merleau-Ponty, and
Emanuel Mounier—philosopher, critic, and controversial jour-
nalist. He was born in Paris in 1924, and educated at the Ecole
Normale Supérieure. He first taught literature in Mexico
and Italy, and then philosophy in Lille and Paris. He is
married, and has three children. Among his books are: *Pour
l'Italie* (1958), *Le Style du Gènèral* (1959), and two volumes
of the *Histoire de la philosophie occidentale,* which are pres-
ently being translated into English. His most recent tract,
Without Marx or Jesus, which attracted world-wide comment,
has just been published in the United States. He writes a
regular column for the Paris news-weekly, *l'Express.*